Calling All Superhero

C000181718

Calling All Superheroes highlights the enormous potential of superhero play in supporting learning and development in early childhood. Using examples from practice, it provides guidance on how to effectively manage and implement superhero play and set appropriate boundaries in early years settings and schools.

Illustrated with engaging photographs and case studies, the book gives ideas about how superhero play can be used to promote positive values and teach children essential life skills. Offering practical strategies and questions for reflection designed to facilitate further development, chapters address important topics and challenges such as:

- Child development, the characteristics of effective learning and the benefits of superhero play, including making sense of right and wrong and increasing moral awareness
- How to broach difficult themes such as death, killing, weapons, aggressive play and gender-related issues
- Supporting children to recognise everyday heroes and how to find heroic abilities within themselves
- The role of the adults in managing superhero play, engaging parents and creating effective learning environments

Written by a leading expert with 20 years' experience in the early years sector, this book is an essential resource for early years teachers, practitioners and anyone with a keen interest in young children's education and learning.

Tamsin Grimmer is an experienced consultant and trainer, a director of Linden Learning and a lecturer in early years at Bath Spa University. She is based in Wiltshire, UK.

Calling All Superheroes

Supporting and Developing Superhero Play in the Early Years

Tamsin Grimmer

Routledge
Taylor & Francis Group
LONDON AND NEW YORK

First published 2020
by Routledge
2 Park Square, Milton Park, Abingdon, Oxon OX14 4RN

and by Routledge
52 Vanderbilt Avenue, New York, NY 10017

Routledge is an imprint of the Taylor & Francis Group, an informa business

British Library Cataloguing-in-Publication Data
A catalogue record for this book is available from the British Library

Library of Congress Cataloging-in-Publication Data
Names: Grimmer, Tamsin, author.
Title: Calling all superheroes : supporting and developing superhero play in the early years / Tamsin Grimmer.
Description: Abingdon, Oxon ; New York, NY : Routledge, 2019. | Includes bibliographical references.
Identifiers: LCCN 2019013038 (print) | LCCN 2019980175 (ebook) | ISBN 9781138556966 (hbk) | ISBN 9781138556973 (pbk) | ISBN 9781315150543 (ebk)
Subjects: LCSH: Early childhood education--Activity programs. | Role playing in children. | Child development. | Superheroes.
Classification: LCC LB1139.35.A37 G75 2019 (print) | LCC LB1139.35.A37 (ebook) | DDC 372.21--dc23
LC record available at https://lccn.loc.gov/2019013038
LC ebook record available at https://lccn.loc.gov/2019980175

ISBN: 978-1-138-55696-6 (hbk)
ISBN: 978-1-138-55697-3 (pbk)
ISBN: 978-1-315-15054-3 (ebk)

Typeset in Bembo
by Integra Software Services Pvt. Ltd.

Contents

Acknowledgements

This book is dedicated to my own not-so-little-anymore superheroes!

First, I'd like to thank my family and friends and their children for sharing their superhero stories and thoughts with me and for putting up with me during the writing period! A special mention goes to my friend Nicky Hurst, who has helped beyond measure with the table in Appendix 2 and huge thanks to my friend and mentor Kay Mathieson for her contributions and continual reminders to keep smiling.

My wholehearted thanks go to the following settings for sharing their ideas and observations about superhero play with me. Without you, this book would not have come to life:

Bluecoat Nursery

Filton Avenue Nursery School

Martenscroft Nursery School and Children's Centre

Odstock Day Nursery

Our Muddy Footprints

Pebbles Childcare

Pen Green Nursery

Rosendale Primary School and Children's Centre

St Mary's Preschool

St Mary's C of E Primary School

Tick Tock Nursery

Westview Day Nursery

Widcombe Acorns Preschool

The Willows Preschool

Winsor Primary School

In addition, I want to thank Katherine Bate, Dr Christina MacRae, Annie McTavish, Kara Godwin, Sue Martin and Zemirah Jazwierska for their contributions to this book and for our professional discussions. I would also like to thank my EYITT students and colleagues at Bath Spa University who have had to put up with me during the writing process.

Thanks also to the publishing team at David Fulton Publishers who have been very patient and understanding with me.

Last, to my very skilled proofreader (aka Mum) – thank you so much for your patience and suggestions, which have helped get this book into shape.

About the author

Tamsin Grimmer is an experienced and highly regarded early years consultant and trainer. She has been working within education in a variety of roles including early years teacher, advisory teacher, area SENCo, childminder and early years consultant and university lecturer. She is currently a director of Linden Learning and balances her time between consultancy work and lecturing on the Primary and Early Years PGCE at Bath Spa University. She is passionate about young children's learning and development and fascinated by how very young children think. She has a keen interest in early brain development, the different ways in which children learn and how practitioners can support them. She is excited to see new and novel ways of recording and documenting children's learning, has been inspired by the practice she saw in Reggio Emilia, and is particularly interested in play, active learning and early language development.

Tamsin believes that all children deserve practitioners who are inspiring, dynamic, reflective and passionate about their learning. When children have the very best start in their early years, they adopt positive dispositions and attitudes to learning and the primary way to assist with this is through inspiring and motivating those who teach and care for them. In this environment, children thrive and grow.

Tamsin's other books include *Observing and Developing Schematic Behaviour* and *School Readiness and the Characteristics of Effective Learning*. She has just graduated with a Masters' Degree in Early Childhood Education (University of Chester) and her dissertation explored love within an early childhood setting. In her time as a teacher, and later as a childminder, she underwent three very positive Ofsted inspections and demonstrated that she was an excellent and outstanding practitioner. Tamsin also put theory into practice with her three children, who keep her feet firmly on the ground.

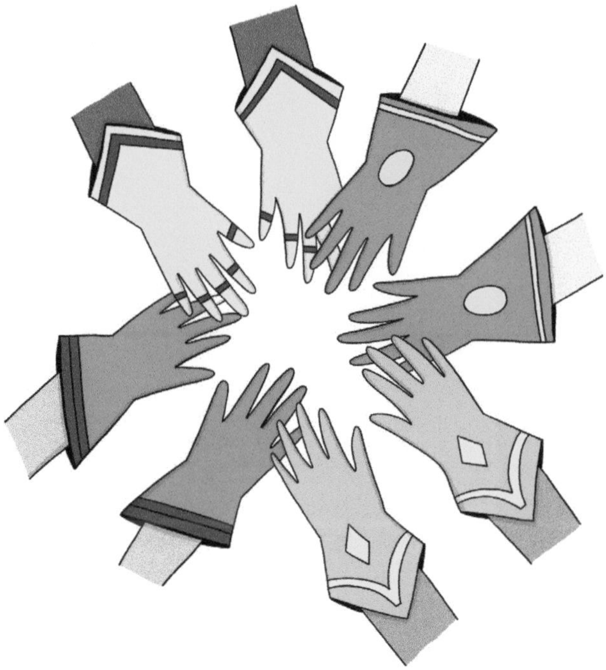

Introduction

Superheroes are a huge part of popular culture. They are instantly recognisable and whatever our view about them, they find their way into our early childhood settings. They are written about in books and are regularly featured in comics, magazines and films or TV programmes and games. In the same way that children can read the "M" for McDonald's before they can read, they can recognise the "S" for Superman or "W" for Wonder Woman. Our children arrive in our settings wearing Batman t-shirts, holding Tree Fu Tom shields or making superhero poses.

Children will develop their play over time and different types of play will go in and out of fashion depending on the latest craze or movie released. At the time of writing, Batman versus Superman, Justice League and Wonder Woman film merchandise is still widely available. Shops are full of film-related dressing-up clothes, toys and books and children can be observed incorporating these characters into their play. In order to understand the children with these interests, it may help practitioners to understand the plots and storylines that accompany them.

This superhero craze is not restricted to children, either. Most recent superhero films (not cartoons) are rated as PG-13 or rated as suitable for children aged over 12 and, in some cases, 15. Many adults also love the whole concept of superheroes and as I write there is a big comic convention in London, which has seen many grown-ups donning a cape or superhero costume. Superheroes are regularly used to advertise products on television, as inspirational characters and as fund-raising mascots. One social enterprise aims to turn the tide on autism by thinking about super-skills instead of autism and thus has adopted superheroes as its publicity device. With literally thousands of superheroes to choose from, you could say that superheroes are super-icons of modern society.

Children regularly engage in play that involves heroes and villains and, within our settings, superheroes come in all sorts of guises and disguises – literally! From Batman to Wonder Woman and from Tree Fu Tom and Go Jetters to doctors and firefighters. Play themes observed frequently include "goodies and baddies", "killing" or "death" and this type of play can often attract boys more than it does girls. Early childhood educators sometimes feel in conflict about whether to embrace this play or to ban it.

This book offers educators an opportunity to explore several issues that rarely get exposure within early childhood settings. We seldom talk about death, killing, gender or fantasy and reality with children. I propose that engaging in superhero play offers us a way into tackling these and other difficult themes. I have drawn on theories of how children learn and researched different play types when writing and appreciate that there are many different perspectives on these themes. As I weave together these different ideas, I hope that those reading this book will draw their own conclusions about how best to support the children they care for within their own setting.

Defining superheroes

Peter Coogan, Director of the Institute for Comic Studies, defines a superhero as: "A heroic character with a selfless, pro-social mission; with superpowers – extraordinary abilities, advanced technology, or highly developed physical, mental, or mystical skills; who has a superhero identity embodied in a codename and iconic costume, which typically express his biography, character, powers, or origin (transformation from ordinary person to superhero)" (Coogan, 2006, p. 30). In addition to this detailed and fantastical definition, the Cambridge Dictionary has a dual definition of a superhero as both, "a character in a film or story who has special strength and uses it to do good things and help other people" and "someone who has done something very brave to help someone else" (2018).

I have considered themes that broadly relate to superheroes, therefore, for the purposes of this book, I am defining superheroes not only as the fictional characters who might rescue the human race from impending peril, but also as people whose actions exceed our expectations, who do good things and help other people. I am also including superheroines within my definition of superheroes so I am intending the term to be gender inclusive. In addition to superheroes, this book also touches on rescuers or characters who are heroic in their mission to save the world and engage in a heroic narrative, e.g. Octonauts and Thunderbirds.

The hero's journey, also known as the monomyth, is the idea, popularised by Campbell (1949), that there is a general pattern that emerges in most superhero stories; the hero goes on a journey, wins a battle and comes back having achieved victory for the good of humankind. Or in Campbell's own words: "A hero ventures forth from the world of common day into a region of supernatural wonder: fabulous forces are there encountered and a decisive victory is won: the hero comes back from this mysterious adventure with the power to bestow boons on his fellow man" (1949, p. 23). We see this monomyth relived again and again within children's superhero play and it could be part of the attraction of engaging in this play.

The benefits of superhero play

What makes superheroes so popular? It is my belief that it is partly the idea that most superheroes are ordinary people, just like us, but with added powers or superhuman abilities. Some became superheroes overnight, by chance or through an accident, which again, may make us feel that, we too, could become heroes. We can imagine how it would feel to have these powers and put ourselves in their shoes, or rather, cape! Superheroes may also be popular because of the predictable monomyth mentioned above and general theme running through the narrative of good overcoming evil, offering children a sense of power in their mostly adult-dominated lives (Rubin and Livesay, 2006).

The whole book is designed to share the benefits of superhero play within different contexts. This type of play is widely seen within early childhood settings and sometimes frowned upon and misunderstood. Occasionally it can be viewed as a type of play that mainly boys engage with and one that is without purpose or intent. Although I have noticed this trend, I have also observed both boys and girls playing superhero-themed games and believe that this play can, indeed, be purposeful and engaging for all.

Each chapter shares ideas about the benefits of superhero play and these are summarised here. Superhero play:

- Offers a great context for imaginative play, fantasy and creativity.
- Provides opportunities for children to develop detailed storylines and narratives.

- Engages even very shy children in exciting storylines.
- Presents children with opportunities to problem solve and resolve conflict.
- Provides opportunities to practise self-regulation and develop emotional intelligence.
- Helps children to explore the triumph of good over evil.
- Offers opportunities to discuss sensitive issues such as death, killing and gender stereotyping with children.
- Opens up conversations with children about everyday superpowers that we can all foster, e.g. resilience, friendship, listening skills.
- Provides plenty of opportunities for gross and fine motor skills, developing proprioception and is usually very physical and active.
- Presents engaging and imaginative contexts which educators can use to develop children's cognitive skills.

Outline of book

This book is divided into different chapters, each of which picks up on a theme that I have linked to superhero play. I have included a few case studies and photographs to further illustrate and bring the themes covered to life. Each chapter concludes with some questions designed to enable you to reflect on your practice in the light of what you have read. These questions should facilitate you to explore the issues raised in each chapter and further develop your practice.

Chapter 1 explores fantasy play in relation to child development. It considers the notion of fantasy versus reality and real and pretend while highlighting the importance of this type of play for children. The chapter briefly discusses fantasy characters including superheroes and villains and considers the value in this play for young children.

Chapter 2 draws on various pieces of research that have looked into aggressive behaviour in young children. It discusses rough and tumble and weapon play and the benefits and concerns relating to these types of play.

Chapter 3 considers the difficult subject of death and killing. It builds on Chapter 2 and considers examples of how practitioners can respond when they encounter children "killing" others or referring to death in their play. It will draw on evidence from research that explores young children's perceptions of death and dying and considers some practical strategies of how to best approach this sensitive topic and support very young children.

Chapter 4 explores gender in relation to young children and how children begin to understand the concept of gender permanence. It discusses the benefits of engaging boys and girls in superhero play, encouraging collaboration between genders and the importance of ensuring a balance between competent, strong girl superheroes as well as the damsel in distress and male superheroes as well as a boy needing to be rescued … In addition it considers how superhero play can help to reduce the gender gap observed regarding boys achievement in early years settings.

Chapter 5 has been written by my good friend and colleague, Kay Mathieson. She focuses on how we can use superhero play to promote the Prevent duty and British values and considers what they mean for us as an early years community.

Chapter 6 explores in more detail the broad definition of a superhero as someone who achieves greatness when it considers heroes in real life and how we can introduce these to young children. Drawing on true stories of heroism within our society this chapter explores how we can teach children about enabling our actions, big and small, to be heroic.

Chapters 7, 8 and 9 focus more on practice, with Chapter 7 looking at how we can create a learning environment that supports superhero play and Chapter 8 sharing some stories of how early childhood educators have successfully implemented superhero play into their settings. Chapter 9 highlights the importance of a supportive home learning environment (HLE) and considers how to engage effectively with parents and carers.

The final chapter in this book will consider the overall benefits of engaging in superhero play in the early years and how we can encourage children to find their own "superpowers". It summarises the main points of the book and offers suggestions of how to successfully implement superhero play in your setting.

I have also included three appendices, which I hope you will find useful. Appendix 1 is an example of a superhero and aggressive play policy. It is my intention that this would be personalised and tweaked to suit individual settings and contexts. Appendix 2 is a chart summarising the mainstream superheroes you may come across in popular culture. It would be nigh on impossible to create an exhaustive list and superhero fans or comic gurus may criticise the simplistic nature of this chart. However, I hope that it sheds some light onto the context and back story of a few of the most popular characters with whom your children may engage. Appendix 3 is another chart that includes a few of the heroic characters currently depicted by children's television and media. Again, this is not intended to be a fully inclusive list – once you start, where do you stop? Nevertheless, I have attempted to include the more popular characters and those whom your children may come across more readily.

So pop an eye mask on and get ready to explore the world of superheroes and what our children can learn through it.

References

Cambridge Dictionary (2018) Meaning of "superhero". Retrieved from https://dictionary.cambridge.org/dictionary/english/superhero
Campbell, J. (1949) *The Hero with a Thousand Faces*. Princeton, CA: Princeton University Press
Coogan, P. (2006) *Superhero: The Secret Origin of a Genre*. Austin, TX: MonkeyBrain Books
Rubin, L. and Livesay, H. (2006) *International Journal of Play Therapy*, *15*(1), pp. 117–133

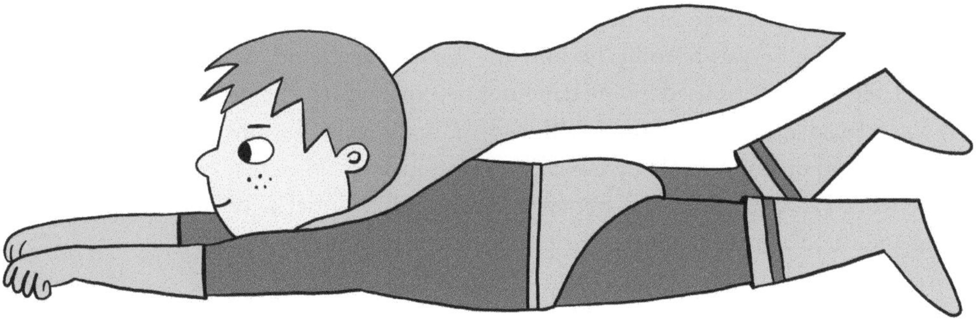

1 "I can fly like Superman!"

The importance of fantasy play in child development

Introduction

When you have a good imagination you are never alone! You can be transported to a world of make-believe where none of your worries exist. You can conjure up friends in any guise and be as good or as naughty as you like! My youngest daughter often goes to an imaginary land, when I asked her what she loved about it she replied: "Vegetables are unhealthy and sweets are healthy!" So, in your imagination, you can eat whatever you like too!

The Oxford Dictionary defines fantasy as: "The faculty or activity of imagining impossible or improbable things" (2019a). This is opposed to the definition of reality which is: "A thing that exists in fact, having previously only existed in one's mind" (2019b). Fantasy play is when children use their imagination and play out scenarios that are impossible or improbable, for example, having superpowers as a superhero. When children pretend about real-life scenarios, for example, pretending they are in a doctor's surgery, this would be called "sociodramatic" play and it is explored in Chapter 6. However, for the purposes of this chapter, I am including all pretence and imaginative play within a broader definition of fantasy play.

Children are excellent players and do not distinguish between fantasy and reality play. They move easily between the two. When one of my daughters was nearly three, I asked her how she hurt her hand and she said: "I went into a deep dark wood with my mummy and I saw a bear and he hurt my hand." I asked if he was a friendly bear and she replied: "Yes, he was friendly, he hurt my hand in accident!" The hurt on her hand was real, the fantasy was used by my daughter to explain how she became hurt and all of this was relayed as fact. Imaginings within the fantasy realm also invoke real feelings, so if we feel good during this play, we will have a positive emotion that outlives the fantasy (Bettleheim, 1975). A child who exclaims "I can fly like Superman!" feels powerful and strong and these are real feelings, albeit ones that stem from fantasy.

Keeping it real, yet encouraging pretence!

Within early childhood education (ECE) we are mindful of the importance of starting with concrete, hands-on, real experiences when working with young children. When we relate concepts and themes to children's own interests we start with the premise that children are competent and knowledgeable and we can build on their prior knowledge and experience. Sometimes we may want to introduce a concept or theme that is totally new to our children and this is when it is vital that we begin with hands-on, real-life examples for the children to explore with their senses.

Yet, while keeping it real, we must also encourage pretence and fantasy play. This type of play feeds children's creativity and helps them to use their imagination. It is a natural way for children to play and we must engage in this with young children. Within our homes, there is often a mixture of real and pretend as many cultures celebrate characters such as Father Christmas and the tooth fairy. These figures are validated by real events and tangible evidence in the form of presents, money or sweets. Many educators naturally incorporate elements of pretence into their settings, which also keeps magic alive. I have tried to do this within my own practice and been inspired by great authors such as Vivian Gussin-Paley (1984, 2010) and Jenny Tyrrell (2001).

Case study – Westview

Peter really enjoyed engaging in fantasy play. He had a particular interest in knights and dragons and his key person tapped into this interest. She suggested that they create a castle in the corner of the room and she found a few props such as swords, shields, dragon's costumes, royal clothes, crowns and silver goblets. She ensured that these props were available and waited to see what the children, particularly Peter, would make of these resources. What followed were hours of fantasy play with strong narratives where Peter or his friends were brave knights and princesses, rescuing one another from the fierce dragon. The adults mostly observed this play, occasionally role modelling how to "fight" a dragon or helping the children to develop more props.

The development of fantasy play

Young children begin pretend play from around 18 months of age and this develops into more refined role play, real or fictional at about three years old (German and Leslie, 2001). However, by around six years, most children have still not fully grasped the difference between knowing something and believing it. Thus early childhood educators are working with children who are learning to distinguish between fantasy and reality, pretend and real. There will be times when these lines are very blurred. You only need to have observed children playing a make-believe game to know that they are fully engrossed in this play, they *are* that character at that moment, in their minds they are not pretending. I was reminded of this recently when I asked my youngest daughter if she was pretending to be the doctor: "No", she replied, "I *am* a doctor!" That certainly put me in my place and I was left in no doubt about how seriously fantasy and make-believe play is taken by children.

Kitson (2010) suggests that, after approximately seven years, if fantasy play is not actively encouraged it slowly diminishes. One way that we can keep the magic of fantasy play alive is through pretence and superhero play. These themes continue to engage older children, teenagers and adults alike, as demonstrated by the amount of media attention dedicated to superheroes. Pretence is the ability to play with an object as if it were something else or take on a role as another person. There are considerable overlaps with fantasy play, which is linked with the improbable and impossible; however, pretending can be more closely linked to reality. Children rarely distinguish between the two and that's OK. Let's think about what this looks like for children.

Bea, 18 months, picks up the teapot in one hand and a jug in the other hand. She imagines she is pouring tea from the teapot into a cup on the tray. Bea offers the teapot to her Grandad who is sitting nearby. She tips her hand holding the teapot to pour tea into his hand which holds an imaginary cup. Bea is incredibly knowledgeable about how to engage with this play, imitating her sisters and the adults around her.

Bea is pretending to pour the tea from the teapot into the cup, so she needs to imagine that there is a liquid in the teapot and needs the fine motor control to "pour" the tea. She is using her imagination and is able to pretend that the tea is in the pot and then the cup ... She is also capable of imagining and engaging with an invisible cup when she pours tea for her Grandad. Children are readily able to move between fantasy, reality and pretence within their play, thus they can move from imagining the possible to imagining the improbable in a more fantastical way as seen in the observation of Aiden and Simon.

Case study – Widcombe Acorns

Aiden regularly incorporates elements of fantasy into his play. This often inspires others to also fantasise and Aiden and his friends are regularly overheard discussing their elaborate play themes and planning who is who. He has a keen interest in superheroes and other fantasy characters.

Aiden: "I'm a werewolf that breathes fire." (Breathes out loudly to demonstrate)

Simon repeats Aiden's phrase: "I'm a werewolf that breathes fire!" He huffs loudly, too. His key person was nearby and asked Aiden, "Are you a goodie or a baddie?"

Aiden: "Goodie. I'm going to make a nice campfire for you. You could roast some marshmallows to eat and share them with your friends."

Aiden "breathes fire" on the floor in front of them and the adult pretends to toast marshmallows on a stick, offering the stick to a child: "Would you like a marshmallow?"

Aiden takes a pretend marshmallow: "Yum, yum, yum in my tum, tum, tum!"

The adult offers one to Simon. Simon takes a pretend marshmallow and says "Yummy."

Adult: "Careful, they're hot – blow on them!"

Aiden replies, "But I've got fire!" He breathes out fire again to demonstrate.

Adult: "You've got fire so you don't need to worry about getting your mouth burned?"

Aiden: "No 'coz we've got fire."

Aiden and Simon move easily between the fantasy of being werewolves and breathing fire to the pretence of toasting marshmallows on the fire and the notions of reality in potentially burning their mouths on the hot marshmallows. Ultimately, it doesn't matter whether children are engaging in play that is grounded in reality or play that stems from fantasy, the important thing for educators to remember is to value this play as an important part of child development. Research has suggested that children who play more fantasy games and engage in a greater number of pretence games are less likely to confuse real and pretend (Sharon and Woolley, 2004). This links with the Piagetian view that children engaging in imaginative and fantasy play add to their understanding and knowledge about the real world.

Children have the ability to easily engage in magical thinking and play with possible and impossible concepts. Many great inventions and theorists who have changed our society began with imaginative or fanciful ideas. These imaginings when developed have turned the impossible into the possible. Einstein held fantasy and imagination in very high regard and suggested that they are more important than knowledge: "Knowledge is limited. Imagination encircles the world" (1929). Thus fantastical thinking is an important attribute and should be actively encouraged within our settings.

Case study – Pebbles childcare

As part of our Chinese New Year celebrations this year, we focused on dragons throughout the festival. This mapped across into the children's free play as two children self-selected these fabrics and asked for them to be tied around their shoulders as they began to flap their arms, roaring, squealing and "breathing" fire as they initiated and developed their own dragon role play. This play combined real elements relating to the Chinese New Year celebrations and fantasy elements as the children became the dragons.

There are many noted benefits for children engaging in this type of fantasy and make-believe play. It:

- Encourages imagination and creativity.
- Builds children's confidence as they experience the freedom to "be" whomever or whatever they want to be.
- Enables children to deal with real-life scenarios in a safe environment.
- Provides an opportunity for children to play games involving social rules, cooperation and collaboration.
- Encourages children to empathise with others.
- Offers children a place to escape from the real world.
- Usually involves a narrative and acts as a type of therapy as children talk through scenarios and possibilities.
- Helps children to deal with changes in their lives.
- Allows children an element of control in their lives – e.g. they can put toppings on a pizza that their parent wouldn't normally allow!
- Improves children's language and communication skills and is a great opportunity for extending children's vocabulary.

- Provides an opportunity for children to negotiate roles and understand rules and boundaries.
- Allows children to problem solve and resolve conflicts themselves.
- Counters stereotypes and discrimination as boys can play at being a mummy and girls at being superman.
- Offers opportunities for children to explore different emotions and practice emotional control and self-regulation.
- Nurtures children's dispositions such as resilience, perseverance and a "can-do" attitude.
- Develops children's cognitive skills and provides opportunities for literacy and numeracy.
- Enhances children's understanding of the world and how things work.
- Allows children to practise fine and gross motor skills.
- Is fun! As educators we are always looking for the purposes in play – we should value this play intrinsically!

Smilansky and Sheftaya (1990, p. 22) introduce six elements that should be present within fantasy and sociodramatic play:

1 Imitative role play – the child undertakes a make-believe role and expresses it in imitative action and/or verbalisation.

2 Make-believe with regard to toys – movements or verbal declarations and/or materials or toys that are not replicas of the object itself are substituted for real objects.

3 Verbal make-believe with regard to actions and situations – verbal descriptions or declarations are substituted for actions or situations.

4 Persistence in role play – the child continues within a role or play theme for a period of at least 10 minutes.

5 Interaction – at least two players interact within the context of the play episode.

6 Verbal communication – there is some verbal interaction related to the play episode.

The authors suggest that, for sociodramatic play, all six of these elements should be present, however, the first four are also components of fantasy play. So a child who has donned a cape and mask and engages in this narrative for 10 minutes or more is engaging in fantasy play.

Distinguishing between fantasy and reality

Young children are developing an understanding of what is real and what is not. Sharon and Woolley refer to the "basic human condition" of attempting to define fantasy and reality and refer to various studies demonstrating that children can distinguish between real objects and images or thoughts and thus between fantasy and reality (2004). Taylor and Howell refer to two different types of fantasy, the first is "withdrawal", when a child may retreat into a make-believe world and the second is when the child confuses reality and fantasy due to a lack of understanding of the world. They researched the latter and found that three-year-olds had a fairly poor ability to distinguish between reality and fantasy and five-year-olds fared much better, with four-year-olds somewhere in between (1973). Sharon and Woolley go on to suggest that children have an additional category of "unsure" when judging between fantasy and reality. This high level of uncertainty can support their understanding further and act like a bridge as they grow and develop blurring the lines between the two camps (2004).

However, other research suggests that children do have a clear understanding of what is real and use their, sometimes limited, knowledge about how the world works in reality to make predictions and assumptions in their pretend play. For example, Lane et al. (2016) discuss a two-year-old child engaging in pretend play pouring tea, in a similar way to Bea above. The child will apply her understanding about how the liquid would pour downwards and could spill onto the pretend situation. This and other such experiments led them to conclude that children's beliefs and imaginings are aligned with reality rather than being permeated with fantasy and impossibilities. Thus children's fantasy play may, in fact, be closely linked with their experiences in reality and therefore are not fantastical at all. However, Cook and Sobel found that children's judgements about what is real versus fantasy is not limited solely to their first-hand experiences (2011), which adds weight to the thinking that children can indeed fantasise and imagine things outside their immediate world. Anecdotal evidence from my own experience aligns with Cook and Sobel's view as I have found that children are very capable of imagining things that are outside their own experience or are fantastical in nature. An example of this stems back to my teaching days. We had a class teddy that used to visit the children's houses at the weekend. The reception aged children grew very attached to "Billy Bear" and would often make him presents and talk to him in the classroom. Billy became part of our class and regularly joined us for teaching sessions. Billy also had a birthday party. We shared some party food with him and I noticed that he hadn't touched it, I asked Billy if he was feeling OK and one of children gently took me to one side and whispered in my ear: "You know he's not actually real Miss ..." These children treated Billy as a real companion, shared stories with him and even shared their food, but if asked, I think they were in no doubt that he was, in fact, a teddy bear. However, this didn't make the experience of playing with Billy any less real for them.

Papatheodorou and Gill value fantasy play as they recommend that early educators should use fantasy characters that children celebrate or play with to give them "opportunities and rich environments where children will use their imagination and think in images and similes to promote reasoning and rational thinking" (2001, p. 92). Hence fantasy play can enhance children's learning.

Case study – St Mary's Primary School

When the reception class children arrived at school one morning they were in for a big surprize! Who could have left these footprints? We thought about their size and guessed they might have been left by a dinosaur! As you can imagine the children were enthralled and this simple starting point led to lots of child-initiated fantasy play and some adult-led learning. Throughout this theme, the class ended up thinking about size and measurement, carnivores and herbivores and reasons why the dinosaurs became extinct. The teachers linked this with ecology in terms of recycling and turning off lights and playing our part to help save the planet so that no more animals would die out. Children were using their imaginations as well as reasoning and rational thinking to explain the footprints and develop their understanding of the various subjects covered throughout this project.

Research into fantasy play often looks at something called "fantasy orientation". Although there is no official scale for this, children who are more inclined to engage in fantasy play than others would be described as having a high fantasy orientation (Sharon and Woolley, 2004). Research also suggests that there are many benefits for these children such as, better emotion regulation skills and greater executive function (Gilpin, Brown and Pierucci, 2015; Pierucci et al., 2014). This is because these children have had the opportunity to practise these skills within their play. They have felt powerful and strong by pretending to be a strong character like a superhero, knight or firefighter. My oldest daughter remembers regularly dressing up in a particular costume and becoming a pirate queen. She said it not only made her feel happy but also powerful because, in her view, pirates are strong and queens are powerful, therefore this combined the two. Thus superhero play empowers children to be powerful in ways that they cannot in reality (Bauer and Dettore, 1997).

Tyrrell shares many stories of how engaging in fantasy play has enhanced the learning in her classroom yet worries that in our factual world where television programmes and technology leave little to the imagination, the ability of children to make believe might be decreasing (2001). Adults need to acknowledge that children see the world differently and recognise the value of "magic" in childhood. Thus a challenge for early childhood educators is to keep the magic alive.

The role of technology in fantasy play

Technology can in itself appear to have "magic qualities, where things can happen at the touch of a button" (Kennington, 2011, p. 1) and children are attracted to this medium. Although I am wary of using too much technology with young children, as they experience a lot outside early childhood settings, I do believe that there can be a place for technological tools and digital technologies to support children's learning and development. One such purpose is fantasy play as children encounter superhero characters in the media and love to recreate these roles in fantasy play. In addition, many electronic games require the user to role play, imagine and understand the rules of the game.

In their research, Sobel and Lillard found that children understood that pretending involved using their mind and that this understanding was strengthened when their pretence involved fantasy figures (2001). For example, if children were asked to pretend to be a stick they felt this involved their bodies and action, however, when asked to pretend to be a magic wand, they acknowledged that this pretence involved their minds as well as their bodies and when they were asked to pretend to be a character from the media their understanding of pretence was strengthened even further. They suggest that this could be because they have encountered these characters in different contexts, mostly involving technology, rather than purely encountering the characters/objects in reality. Within television programmes, video games and films, characters can contravene the laws of the real world. We see animals walking and talking, superheroes flying and in their view, children understand this to be fantasy, concluding that, "fantasy and pretence could bridge the gap between children's understanding of the fantasy/reality distinction and pretence representations" (Sobel and Lillard, 2001, p. 96). In other words, the characters that children are encountering through digital media are reaffirming children's understanding of reality and fantasy as they fully understand that these characters are fantastical.

Ruckenstein noted that children were naturally able to move between the real world and the virtual world competently, perhaps more so than many adults give them credit for (2010). Sharon and Woolley concur with this view stating that: "Children have a more developed appreciation of the boundary between fantasy and reality than is often supposed" (2004, p. 293). However, other research into young children's understanding of television images being real or representational, found that children go through various developmental stages, with younger children assuming what they see on television is real and tangible and as children get older so their understanding of television as representing real and fictional objects and events grows (Flavell et al., 1990).

Research has also found that children often watch something on television and then immediately engage in role play based on what they have seen (Palaiologou, 2016). I have observed this myself at home with my own children and also within settings where children are bringing in ideas for characters or storylines based on their viewing habits. The percentage of children who do this reduces as they get older, however, these examples demonstrate that children can combine technology and fantasy play successfully. Many superheroes (e.g. Superman, Spider-Man, Batman etc.) have cartoon versions of their adventures and comics and books aimed at younger viewers and readers. There is a fabulous website called commonsensemedia.org (2018) that aims to help parents and educators make informed decisions to enable children to "thrive in a world of media and technology". This is definitely worth a look.

Case study – Widcombe Acorns

Three children were playing outside and had taken on characters from the children's cartoon PJ Masks.
Aiden: "We can't have a story time because Luna Girl has taken all the books!"
Maddie: "Stop Luna Girl because Luna Girl takes everything!"
Simon: "She even takes the moon!"
Maddie: "And she has a moon ball!"
Aiden: "And she runs super-fast."

All three children run off together.
Aiden shouts: "We can run super-fast against baddies!"
Maddie: "I can run ..."
Simon: "That way!"
Aiden: "I'm going to stop Luna Girl and be camouflaged."
Simon: "Come on! Camouflaged and super-speedy!"
Aiden: "Run like this!" Aiden runs off shouting: "So long Luna Girl!"

This play continued for about 15 minutes and developed with them driving Catboy's Cat Car, fighting off another character called Romeo and eventually finding all the books that Luna Girl had stolen and returning them. The children remained in character for the duration of the game and bounced ideas off one another, using their knowledge of the characters and programme to enhance their play.

Children regularly use their knowledge of television characters and incorporate these into their play and therefore digital media can play a role in enhancing children's fantasy narratives. However, a word of caution, if the technology is leading the play, then the children may not be initiating or directing it and it is unlikely to be open-ended play that encourages children's creativity and fantastical thinking. Therefore I urge you to consider the role that technology should or should not have in relation to fantasy play within your own setting.

Imaginary friends

Two of my three children have had imaginary friends at various points in their young lives. At one stage, we even had to lay the table so that "Mr Bat" could sit and eat with us. We describe children as having imaginary friends when they use their imagination to engage in pretend play with another being who is a product of their imagination. These friends could take any form and having such friends is not a cause for concern and should not be treated as such. For many children their toys are "real" to them and fulfil the place that an imaginary friend would take in a more tangible way. However, setting a place for a toy feels more socially acceptable somehow.

Imaginary friends are part of "normal" (I hate that word!) child development and if a child has an imaginary friend this is evidence of a healthy and active imagination (Bouldin, 2006). Children can practise interacting with others socially with their imaginary friend and these friends may last for a short or long period of time. Children who have had imaginary friends may appear less shy and grow up to be more social than other children. It is important to accept their imaginary friend, so do set a place at the table for them or clip them into their (imaginary) car seat. As imaginary friends are controlled by the child, they should not bully them or act in an unkind way to the child. Very occasionally, imaginary friends can be an insight into another issue, so if you have any concerns encourage the child's parents to talk it over it with a health visitor or GP.

What does this mean in practice?

It is generally accepted that one way that children learn is through imitation and when adults role model specific behaviours, children will frequently choose to copy them. When practitioners interact with a group of children playing Spider-Man, they may imagine webs bursting from their hands and "climb up" imaginary walls to help re-enact the storyline. The adults are taking on a role, often portraying the character more accurately than the child, due to their experience of this character. Thus providing the children with another role model for them to imitate demonstrating how Spider-Man would act.

Children need to "imitate, practise and consolidate" new knowledge about the social world that they live in (Buchan, 2013, p. 13) and role play and fantasy play are vital elements alongside time and resources for this to happen. The fantasy play stage provides opportunities for children to practise their language and social interactions as: "Pretend play offers children a safe place to be wrong about just about everything and for it to be OK" (Buchan, 2013, p. 50). In addition to this, research suggests that children who have big feelings or who are struggling with an aspect of their life may feel unable to tell an adult, yet can play out these feelings and scenarios through pretence and fantasy (Linn, 2008).

Research by Lobman (2003, 2005) found that adults disrupted play less when they were co-players like in the Spider-Man example above, and not simply observing or facilitating the play, however, it has been argued that: "During role and imaginary play, the distance between the children and the nearest educator is the largest. Role play seems to be the most alive when there are no educators interfering with it!" (Reunamo et al., 2013, p. 301). Sometimes parents and educators who control children's play and pretence activities are to a certain extent inhibiting their children from deeper and more independent play scenarios (Melzer and Palermo, 2016). This means that some children choose freedom from adults in order to play independently and fantasy play scenarios offer children opportunities to be autonomous and away from the adults. Our role as an educator is to be sensitive to this play, observe closely and decide when to interact and role model or become a co-player and when to hold back and remain an observer. There could be opportunities for both interaction with the children and remaining on the outside within a single play episode.

Practical ideas of how to support children with fantasy play:

- Offer children a language-rich environment.
- Read and share stories that encourage children to use their imaginations.
- Create provocations that inspire children to question, think, ponder and imagine.
- Provide open-ended resources that require children to use their imagination in order to develop themes and opportunities for loose parts play.
- Equip role play areas with large pieces of material, hats, old clothes, non-specific costumes and capes as well as props such as doctor's case, firefighter's helmet etc.
- Offer resources to support role play and sociodramatic play scenarios (e.g. hairdresser, Post Office, cafe, supermarket) and provide open access to graphics areas where children can create their own props, signs and symbols to aid their fantasy narrative.
- Introduce the children to various soft toys, puppets, dolls and small-world play characters so that they can incorporate these into their play.
- Use fantasy as a medium to engage children within your own teaching.
- Role model using different objects for different purposes, e.g. "We could use umbrellas as wheels for our bus!"
- Become a "fantasy play spotter" and develop ways of extending children's play narratives based on these interests.
- Model playing fantasy games and taking on roles in your play with children.
- Encourage children to create fantastical stories, the more absurd the better!
- Share in "What if . . ." or "Would you rather" discussions with the children, e.g. "What if lamp posts were made of chocolate?" or "Would you rather swim in custard or jump over a moon?"
- Accept and value children's fantasy play, positively commenting about it to both children and parents.

In summary

Children have wonderful imaginations and are able to move between fantasy and real worlds, so it is vital that early years practitioners enable children to do this. Through fantasy and magical play, children can reside in a world of fairies, unicorns, dragons and superheroes. This fantasy realm is a place of laughter, of fun, of mischief and most definitely of learning. Papatheodorou and Gill warn us against formalising early childhood "to an extent to forget that the experience of childhood is magical" (2001, p. 92). It is our duty to keep fantastical thinking alive and superhero play in its widest context does just that.

I will leave the last word in this chapter to Susan Isaacs who, in 1931, had no idea what the various advances of the 21st century would bring for young children. She said:

> Let the child play and sing and dance to his heart's content. Let him make-believe and act and draw and dig. Let him read of fairies and ogres and princes and sleeping beauties. But let us not deny his active interest in the real when he shows it.
>
> (Isaacs, 1931, p. 7)

Questions for reflection

1 How can you support children to develop an understanding of real and pretend, while allowing them to engage in age appropriate fantasy play?
2 In what ways does society complicate children's understanding of fantasy figures?
3 What do you see as your role in relation to supporting children's fantasy play?

References

Bauer, K. L. and Dettore, E. (1997) Superhero play: what's a teacher to do? *Early Childhood Education Journal, 25*(1), pp. 17–21

Bettleheim, B. (1975) *The Uses of Enchantment: The Meaning and Importance of Fairy Tales*. New York: Vintage Books

Bouldin, P. (2006) An investigation of the fantasy predisposition and fantasy style of children with imaginary companions, *Journal of Genetic Psychology, 167*(1), pp. 17–29

Buchan, T. (2013) *The Social Child. Laying the Foundations of Relationships and Language.* Oxford: Routledge

Common Sense Media (2018) Retrieved from https://www.commonsensemedia.org/about-us/our-mission

Cook, C. and Sobel, D. (2011) Children's beliefs about the fantasy/reality status of hypothesized machines, *Developmental Science*, *14*(1),pp. 1–8

Einstein, A. (1929) As quoted in "What life means to Einstein: an interview by George Sylvester Viereck" in *The Saturday Evening Post* (26 October) Retrieved from http://www.saturdayeveningpost.com/wp-content/uploads/satevepost/ what_life_means_to_einstein.pdf

Flavell, J., Flavell, E., Green, F. and Korfmacher, J. (1990) Do children think of television images as pictures or real objects? *Journal of Broadcasting and Electronic Media*, *34*(4), pp. 399–419

German, T. and Leslie, A. (2001) Children's inferences from "knowing" to "pretending" and "believing", *British Journal of Developmental Psychology*, *19*, pp. 59–83

Gilpin, A., Brown, M. and Pierucci, J. (2015) Relations between fantasy orientation and emotion regulation in preschool, *Early Education and Development*, *26*(7), pp. 920–932

Gussin-Paley, V. (1984) *Boys and Girls. Superheroes in the Doll Corner.* Chicago, IL: University of Chicago Press

Gussin-Paley, V. (2010) *The Boy on the Beach. Building Community through Play.* London: University of Chicago Press

Isaacs, S. (1931) The child as a scientist. *The Spectator*, 8 August, pp. 6–7

Kennington, L. (2011) Young children and technology. Early education learning together series, 1–2. Retrieved from https://www.early-education.org.uk/young-children-and-technology

Kitson, N. (2010) Children's fantasy role play – why adults should join in. In Moyles, J. (Ed.) *The Excellence of Play*. London: McGraw-Hill

Lane, J., Ronfard, S., Francioli, S. and Harris, P. (2016) Children's imagination and belief: prone to flights of fancy or grounded in reality? *Cognition*, *152*, pp. 127–140

Linn, S. (2008) *The Case for Make Believe: Saving Play in a Commercialized World.* New York: New Press

Lobman, C. (2003) The bugs are coming! Improvisation and early childhood teaching, *Young Children*, *58*(3), pp. 18–23

Lobman, C. (2005) "Yes and": the uses of improvisation for early childhood professional development, *Journal of Early Childhood Teacher Education*, *26*(3), pp. 305–319

Melzer, D. and Palermo, C. (2016) "Mommy, you are the Princess and I am the Queen": how preschool children's initiation and language use during pretend play relate to complexity, *Infant and Child Development*, *25*(2), pp. 221–230

Oxford University Press (OUP) (2019a) Definition of "fantasy". Retrieved from https://en.oxforddictionaries.com/definition/fantasy

Oxford University Press (OUP) (2019b) Definition of "reality". Retrieved from https://en.oxforddictionaries.com/definition/reality

Palaiologou, I. (2016) Children under five and digital technologies: implications for early years pedagogy, *European Early Childhood Education Research Journal*, *24*(1), pp. 5–24

Papatheodorou, T. and Gill, J. (2001) Magic/mythic stories and children's development: the case of the Father Christmas story, *Early Childhood Education Research Journal*, *9*(2), pp. 83–96

Pierucci, J., O'Brien, C., McInnis, M., Gilpin, A. and Barber, A. (2014) Fantasy orientation constructs and related executive function development in preschool: developmental benefits to executive functions by being a fantasy-oriented child, *International Journal of Behavioral Development*, *38*(1), pp. 62–69

Reunamo, J., Lee, H., Wu, R., Wang, L., Mau, W. and Lin, C. (2013) Perceiving change in role play, *European Early Childhood Education Research Journal*, *21*(2), pp. 292–305

Ruckenstein, M. (2010) Toying with the world: children, virtual pets and the value of mobility, *Childhood*, *17*(4), pp. 500–513

Sharon, T. and Woolley, J. (2004) Do monsters dream? Young children's understanding of the fantasy/reality distinction, *British Journal of Developmental Psychology, 22*, pp. 293–310

Smilansky, S. and Sheftaya, L. (1990) *Facilitating Play: A Medium for Promoting Cognitive, Sociocultural and Academic Development in Young Children.* Gaithersburg, MD: Psychosocial and Educational Publications

Sobel, D. and Lillard, A. (2001) The impact of fantasy and action on young children's understanding of pretence, *British Journal of Developmental Psychology, 22*, pp. 85–98

Taylor, B. and Howell, R. (1973) The ability of three-, four-, and five-year-old children to distinguish fantasy from reality, *Journal of Genetic Psychology, 122*, pp. 315–318

Tyrrell, J. (2001) *The Power of Fantasy in Early Learning.* London: Routledge

2 "I'm going to make a gun!"

Exploring aggression and violent play

Introduction

As an early years consultant and university lecturer, I am regularly asked my opinion about violent or aggressive play and, more specifically, my view on gun play. The conversation usually begins like this: "What are your views on aggressive play? Should I ban it or run with it? I have a group of children, mainly boys, who can turn anything into a gun, so even when there are no toy guns or weapons, they manage to make a 'zapper' out of a block or will pick up a stick and start 'shooting' each other with it."

Does this sound familiar? These questions are not new, but, if anything, have increased in frequency over the years. They have certainly grown in relevance due to more weapon- (knife)- related crime being recorded within society and violent behaviour having escalated in recent years (Office for National Statistics, 2018). Are we contributing to this rise in violent behaviour because of our input with young children or can we combat it and offer children an alternative perspective?

Violent themes regularly find their way into children's play and this could be attributed to many influences for example, video games, television, books and, sadly, real-life violence that they see. Thus weapon play or aggressive play will do nothing to limit their exposure to these things from societal influences. Every day the news reports item after item that in some way share stories of violence, aggressive behaviour and abuse. In addition, many children's programmes and cartoons depict violence and aggression, albeit in a watered-down fashion. It would be nigh on impossible to protect children or shelter them from these influences. In one sense, we have attempted to do this in our own home – if the news begins while the radio is on, we turn the volume down until it goes back to music. Despite these habits, our own children create stick guns, enjoy rough and tumble play, act aggressively towards one another and enjoy a water-shooting match as much as the next child!

Research shows that aggressive play is relatively common and a natural occurrence and episodes of this type of play usually diminish with age (Cummings, Iannotti and Zahn-Waxler, 1989; Tremblay, 2000). For the purposes of this chapter, I am considering aggressive play widely and, as its name suggests, I am viewing it as a type of play. Aggressive play includes rough and tumble, play fighting, throwing toys or acting aggressively towards another child. I am distinguishing it from violence and will share my understanding of the differences later in the chapter. I will also offer ideas and comments intended to encourage reflection on practice and how we react to these types of play.

For some parents and practitioners, the answer is to immediately ban toy weapons and put a stop to any play that becomes too aggressive; Chapter 8 considers this idea in detail. I propose that rather than focusing on toys and placing the blame of our increase in societal violence on children growing up with more exposure to violence, we should be looking at how we, as parents and educators, are engaging with children and talking about these issues. Children are growing up in the real world and not everyone plays nicely. Rough play gives us an opportunity to learn how to respond, to keep ourselves safe, to resolve conflicts and even to protect ourselves. Reprimanding children for playing in natural and aggressive ways could cause a barrier between adults and children, rather than allowing for open communication and maximising opportunities to teach life skills.

Rough and tumble play

In schools and other settings, we care for the children in the best way we know how and their wellbeing is our highest priority. We understand the importance of building secure attachments with children and we strive to follow their interests and cater for their individual needs. If a child cries we tend to them, if they need a nappy change, we change it, if they are hungry we feed them, if they need reassurance, we reassure them. If they need a hug or a cuddle, we cuddle them – there should be no hesitation. Why is it, when they need to rough and tumble, we are horrified and try to redirect their attention elsewhere?

Take a moment to think back to your own childhood. What sorts of games can you remember playing? Did they ever involve running, chasing, being chased, tickling, wrestling or fighting baddies? Did your play make links with the popular culture of the time? For me, the answers to both these questions are yes. Now consider what you were learning through playing in these ways? What skills were you practising? Perhaps socialising? How to take risks or set limits? Were you learning about friendship and family roles? Rough and tumble play is a natural thing for children to want to engage in. We need to work out for ourselves how we can enable this play while setting appropriate limits that keep children safe.

Case study – Pebbles childcare

What started as an innocent cuddle between our eldest and youngest child quickly escalated into a "beach school bundle" with the younger children becoming monsters trying to eat the older child who was on the bottom of the bundle! The girls spent over five minutes like this, tickling one another, roaring like monsters and the sound of their hysterical laughter was beautiful!

In our setting, rough and tumble play is an integral part of learning and development, particularly with the boys and, in our opinion, restricting this play will only cause children to behave aggressively. Learning about boundaries and physical limits is a vital experience and as long as all participants are happy to be involved then children need the chance to explore and test these boundaries within a safe and controlled environment.

Rough and tumble play is very physical and active and can involve actions such as wrestling, tickling, pinning others down, pouncing, climbing or sitting on each other, "bundles" and chasing games like "tag" and "it". It could be argued that play fighting is also a form of rough and tumble play. Having said this, Huber (2017) suggests that the term rough and tumble is in itself misleading because it is not always rough and doesn't always involve tumbling! When you observe children playing in this way, you will hear lots of giggling and laughing and you will see children smiling and grinning. If the rough and tumble includes a fantasy narrative, you may also observe some pretence and imaginative storytelling as in the example above from Pebbles childcare. Rough and tumble play can be misinterpreted by adults as violent behaviour. However, children need this physically active play as it enhances their development and therefore we need to ensure that children have time to rough and tumble in a safe environment.

Rough and tumble play is regularly linked to fantasy play or pretence and can involve rule negotiation and concepts of fairness and justice. It can support children to develop these ideas further throughout their lives. There are indeed many other benefits for children who engage in rough and tumble play.

Rough and tumble play:

- Helps to develop our sense of proprioception, working out where our bodies are in relation to space and people around us.
- Is a very social activity that contributes to our understanding of social rules.
- Improves self-regulation as children need to learn when to stop and to balance what they want with the desires of others.
- Develops empathy and helps with theory of mind as children learn that other people have feelings and emotions that might be different from their own.
- Enables children to safely manage risk for themselves.
- Allows children to manage aggressive feelings in a safe environment.
- Develops gross motor skills and physical dexterity.
- Offers children the opportunity to win and not gloat or lose and accept defeat graciously.
- Provides an opportunity for children to use their imaginations as they create their narratives.
- Allows children to bond with adults and other children.
- Is enjoyable for those who participate.
- Enables children to learn about pain in an appropriate way as "little cuts and bruises" are an important part of our survival instinct. (Hughes, 2012, p. 126)

Jarvis and George (2010) talk about rough and tumble play as being vital for healthy child development and Huber (2017) strongly argues that children need rigorous physical play and educators should be aware of the whole child, including the need for movement, the whole day. However, despite the many benefits, many early childhood educators do not feel comfortable with this play. There are usually several anxieties that educators express when responding to rough and tumble play. First, they fear that, if a child gets hurt or upset, they may be blamed for allowing this play to happen, second, they feel that this type of play is not effective practice and therefore shouldn't be encouraged and, third, they are concerned that rough and tumble play will lead to real fighting and violence.

These ideas are understandable and we need to unpick them if we are to overcome such thoughts and make an informed decision about our own response to this play in our settings. It can sometimes help to ask ourselves: "What is the worst that can happen?" and "Can I put measures in place to lower the likelihood of this happening?" This is not only about risk assessment, but also about understanding the dynamics of the group and knowing the children really well so that you can respond sensitively when needed. Scott and Panksepp (2003) note that for preschool-aged children, rough and tumble play leads to real fighting less than 1% of the time, so this should not be a barrier to allowing such play. They proposed that although this play can appear aggressive, it should not be considered in this way, as they found a distinct absence of aggression throughout their research. They also identified that it is commonplace for children aged between three and six years to have an urge to engage in rough and tumble activities and this is part of typical development.

Perhaps some educators worry about joining in with this play because of its close physical aspects. Research has shown that young children need to touch and be touched (Bergnehr and Cekaite, 2018), however, many adults are wary of touching the children in their care, for fear of its being misinterpreted (Piper and Smith, 2003). Early childhood educators need to stand firm in the knowledge of what is right for their young children and ensure that their setting's policies also talk about positive touch and their rationale for close physical relationships that include appropriate touch. Huber offers some great advice: whenever possible, let the child decide who touches them, for example, by asking "Do you want a hug?" or "Can we rough and tumble together?" (2017). This is not only respectful to the child, but also a great habit for a child to learn that adults need permission to touch them and they are in control of their body.

Even if more aggressive play is permissible in terms of policy, it is often "taboo in practice" (Rosen, 2015, p. 246) and this could be because of the tension that practitioners experience when encountering this type of play, when adults may worry about other people's perceptions. This is a real concern, as visitors to our settings may not fully understand our rationale for allowing children to play more aggressively. Inspectors, parents and other people visiting could make judgements based on the snapshot of play that they observe, which could look uncontrolled and purposeless. However, if educators are concerned about what others will think with regards to their pedagogy and amend their practice accordingly, they are not being true to what they believe is right for young children. This may negatively impact the children as they will not have as many opportunities to develop their imaginative play. In addition, imposing rules that encourage or even make the children's play conform to adult expectations could be inappropriate and restrictive. A zero tolerance approach to any sort of aggressive play as discussed in Chapter 8 suppresses children's play and necessitates a huge amount of negative interactions from practitioners who have to actively police play to enforce their rules (Holland, 2003; Rich, 2003).

So what is the way forward? We need to discuss our approach as a team because consistency of response with children is vitally important. Begin with observing the children in our care, then consider which behaviours we find acceptable and which, if any, are unacceptable and discuss how we will intervene in future. It can be helpful to think in terms of: "When a child … adults will …" Ensuring that we initially work at the comfort level where our colleagues who feel least at ease with rough play sit will help to foster our team and not be divisive. Then we can discuss the benefits of permitting this play and although there is no requirement to have a specific policy on aggressive play, it can be helpful to write one that best fits our ethos. It can state our views and rationale clearly for everyone involved, including parents, educators and inspectors and can help us to be consistent in our approach with the children. We can also talk to children about the consequences of their actions and what happens when they behave a certain way. Appendix 1 offers an example of such a policy that can be adapted to suit the needs of individual settings.

Case study – village preschool

In our setting, we observed several children playing superhero games that involved rough and tumble, chasing and aggressive behaviours. We talked to the children about these interests and found that several of them were watching a cartoon called *PJ Masks* and engaging in rough and tumble play at home. We met as a team to share our observations. We are a small team and decided that we wanted to allow this play to continue and began to role model appropriate interactions with the group, but we were worried what the parents would think. So we wrote a letter to the parents on behalf of their children. It went something like this:

Dear Mummy/Daddy,

You might have noticed me dressing up as a superhero lately and sometimes chasing and wrestling with others as part of my play. Sometimes we do this together at home too. My teachers call this rough and tumble play and they say that it is really good for me. It teaches me how to set boundaries and limits, how to feel powerful and strong yet be gentle at the same time and how to be more aware of my own body. They said that we all need to listen to each other to know when it's time to stop playing this way and you can help me to understand how to calm myself down. At home and at preschool, we are a team together making sure that I don't get hurt and don't hurt others too.

Thank you for playing with me and for letting me play these games that I love, Your child.

We received very positive feedback from families, some of whom were unsure about how to respond to this play themselves. Several fathers said that they were really pleased we were allowing this play, because rough and tumble was the main way that they played with their children.

We also wrote a policy for our setting that outlined the benefits of aggressive play and how we as early childhood educators were role modelling and extending this play. We included information about what we would do if we were concerned about threatening or violent behaviour and described the rules and boundaries that we put in place to keep everyone safe. We have seen a reduction in the amount of violent behaviour in our setting as a result of allowing this play to continue. We have even linked into their interest in *PJ Masks* by encouraging children to have "super-hearing" like Catboy or "super-eyesight" like Owlette, helping them to maintain attention and concentration during a session.

Telling the difference between aggressive play and aggressive fighting or violence

Lindon (2001) distinguishes between rough and tumble play and play fighting, however, she insists that these are both very distinct from aggressive fighting. Puppies learn bite control by play biting with their siblings. Biting one another to practise how hard is too hard! Without this practise, it could be argued that a puppy wouldn't know its own strength of bite. This play biting can look scary to an onlooker who doesn't understand the behaviour of puppies, in a similar way, it is crucial as educators that we can tell the difference between play and real in terms of children's aggressive behaviour. In my experience, I have found that men are more able to distinguish between real aggression and aggressive play than women and are more willing to engage in aggressive play with children. This raises an important issue for us within ECE where approximately 98% of educators are female (Simon, Owen and Hollingworth, 2016). Are we denying children the opportunity to engage in rough play simply because the workforce is predominantly female? Chapter 4 explores gender issues in relation to superhero play in more detail.

A colleague of mine, Dr Christina MacRae, observed an interesting episode of play that could have been deemed aggressive or even violent but that she has interpreted using Manning's idea of the minor gesture (Manning, 2016). Through close observation of subtle shifts and changes in gestures, we can tune into children's behaviour and interactions more closely. As part of her research project (MacRae, forthcoming 2019), Christina videoed the action and played it back in slow motion. The slow-motion footage allowed her to pay more attention to the details of the ways that the boys both worked collectively with each other, as well as the way that their bodies were relating to the wall through movement, as described in the case study below. This was an exciting and risky play activity that superficially could have appeared to be violent or aggressive in nature, but, for those boys, was a physically rewarding and a positive social experience.

Case study – Martenscroft Nursery School and Children's Centre

Three boys aged between two and three years were engaged in physical play outside. As the play developed, the children deliberately ran at full speed toward a metal garage wall and bashed into it. Each impact made a loud crashing noise. All three boys had a huge smile on their face as they smashed into the wall clearly communicating their enjoyment in this activity. As they prepared their bodies in anticipation for the impact, they placed both hands, palms facing the garage, in front of them so that the first impact was with their hands. It was as if they were flattening their bodies as they prepared to hit the wall. This necessitated them to exercise very precise proprioceptive awareness, which contributed to their growing physical dexterity. In addition, one of the children who had previously been on the outside of the group became fully integrated into the group during this activity and this could be seen as feeding into his growing social confidence.

It could be argued that play fighting and rough and tumble play are examples of mammalian play where animals playfully switch between being in control and losing control to practise skills they will need later in life. Biben and Suomi (1993, p. 187) describe the two universal, and somewhat stereotypical, "signals of harmless and playful intent" in which primates adopt a "play face", which is an open-mouthed grin and lie on their backs to expose their tummy. The same is true of children; they regularly adopt a "play face" and games will often involve children lying, rolling or wrestling in a position that exposes their tummies or more vulnerable parts. Through playing in these ways and seeking out uncertainty, children are in training for the unexpected events that may occur in their lives (Spinka, Newberry and Bekoff, 2001).

Here are some tips to help you to distinguish between aggressive play and real violence:

- Watch body language and facial expression – are their eyes smiling or are they frowning?
- Listen for laughter, play shouting and giggling, not crying or screaming in pain. Play tends to include higher pitched voices and violence a lower tone and angry sounding words.
- Closely observe the play, listen to any words spoken – is there a narrative? Are the comments personal?
- Are all children consenting to this play and willingly joining in?
- Are there positive rewards for all players – i.e. this is not bullying when one child dominates the play.
- Do stronger children sometimes allow their opponents to win?
- Closely watch the contact: is it unrelenting, hard and harsh (violent) or relatively gentle and playful?
- Do children sometimes change roles or take alternate roles? For example, the chaser starts to be chased.
- Do the children know each other well? Rough and tumble promotes attachments – children tend not to rough and tumble with strangers!
- Count the number of children involved. Violence tends to involve two children, rough and tumble or aggressive play can incorporate several children at once.
- Violent acts often draw a crowd whereas aggressive play does not draw spectators in the same way.
- Ask the children – most children know that rough and tumble or aggressive play is not real fighting. They will tell you if things go too far.

In the light of the many benefits linked to aggressive play, perhaps early childhood educators should focus their efforts on closely observing children in order to recognise the difference between violence and aggressive play. This will enable them to permit this play in appropriate ways and in a safe environment. The educator's role then becomes one of effective supervision, role modelling and close observation to ensure that all children are happy and still consenting to the game.

Weapon play

At the time of writing, Prince George was pictured playing with a toy gun, which has sparked a debate about whether this is a suitable toy for a young royal, with many people questioning the parenting choices of the Duchess of Cambridge. However, Prince George comes from a family with a long tradition of hunting and military service, so it comes as no surprise that the toy of his choice is a gun. It is very typical of children to represent their life experiences within play; however, weapon play is always a controversial issue within ECE and fosters strong opinions on all sides.

Case study – preschool

Sam is crouched down, hiding behind the bushes. He briefly stands up to peer over the top of the bush, scanning the horizon for his friend. "Ne-ow, ne-ow!" Isaac shoots at Sam! Sam screams and quickly crouches down again. "You're dead!", comes the cry from Isaac. Sam stands up again and says: "Missed me. Ne-ow!" He shoots back at Isaac and the firing continues for a few minutes. Then Sam shouts: "Now you're dead – I got you!" Isaac makes a show of being shot in the heart. He clutches his chest and shouts "Nooooo!" falling to the floor! Isaac stands up again and says to Sam, "Now I'm dead let's play zombies ..." "No, let's play that I'm the baddie and you're chasing me ..." Sam runs off before Isaac can reply and Isaac gives chase!

Educators around the world will recognise this level of fantasy play, often played out by boys as one shoots the other and then exclaims: "You're dead!" It is perfectly acceptable for the "dead" child to get up and continue playing. Children do not appear to understand the finality of death, what matters is playing the game and engaging in the fantasy. The next chapter considers children's understanding of death and addresses some of these issues.

When a wrapping paper tube becomes a sword, sticks become bows and arrows and torches become laser guns, banning weapon play is rather tricky! Many children can skilfully turn anything into a weapon and this creativity should be encouraged, not banned. Let's think this through using the analogy of a robot. If a child has a fascination with robots and turns everything she makes into a robot, we would praise her and say isn't it wonderfully imaginative ... However, when a child makes an intricate weapon that can zap, shoot lasers, webs and bullets, we often chastise her and say this is destructive. It could be argued that making a robot differs because robots are not designed to kill, however, children do not see this subtle difference – they hear one message – you like that child and value her interests, but you don't like me or value mine. This can be incredibly damaging to our children, particularly boys, who most regularly engage in weapon play.

Case study – St Mary's Preschool

A small group of boys had a keen interest in Power Rangers and regularly arrived in role in the session. On this occasion, they used plastic screws and nuts to carefully assemble their shooters while discussing the parts they would play and then engaged in a game all about goodies and baddies. Our role within this play was to ensure that these materials were available, scaffold the play, extend the narrative, encourage cooperation, problem solving and conflict resolution.

You may hear children play with power in different ways – just like in the case study from St Mary's Preschool. Some children might play at schools and send children to the headteacher, while others might build a gun, chase and catch a "baddy" or take him to prison. Often this play takes a long time to set up as children talk about what characters they will be, how the plot will pan out, who the baddies are and what they have done. This takes time and lots of active communication and cooperation – which is definitely to be encouraged. The weapon is not the whole story.

Holland considers weapon play in her book *We Don't Play with Guns Here*. She suggests that rather than focus on the weapon, we should consider the child holding it (2003). I think this is a vitally important message. Adults are often unsure of the value in weapon play and many early childhood settings ban this play without a clear rationale as to why. They question whether we should be allowing children to feel that it's fun to shoot someone. Could it be desensitising children to the evil of guns at a young age? Despite these misgivings, in my view banning or discouraging superhero and weapon play disadvantages those children who are so engrossed by it. Instead, we can engage with the play, redirect it positively and use it as an opportunity to foster their imaginations and extend thinking and learning skills. For example, we can teach children the problem-solving technique to conflict resolution, giving them skills that will last them a lifetime (see Chapter 8).

Playing with power themes and weapons can also offer opportunities for playing in groups and cooperating together. Children can be encouraged to express their feelings in a safe and secure environment and taught strategies for managing aggression. They can learn that there is more than one way to resolve conflicts and that actions have consequences. If children do not have the chance to play in this way, they will not have as many opportunities to learn these skills.

One educator said to me: "I cannot think of anything good about a gun and there is no value in gun play because the purpose of a gun is to kill." While I respect, understand and can relate to this viewpoint, I would like to suggest that within children's play, a gun is not designed to actually kill. Children will regularly "shoot" one another, however, research indicates that children do not have the full understanding of what this means (see Chapter 3). In addition, I propose that if we are truly looking at the child behind the weapon that should include valuing any interests that fall outside our own expertise or comfort zones.

The UN Convention on the Rights of the Child (Unicef, 1989) covers children's right to play (Article 31) and protects their freedom of expression (Article 13). It could be argued that limiting children's play choices is directly contravening these articles. In addition, I have discussed gun play with several settings that serve military families and therefore need to have a different approach when it comes to weapons – they cannot dismiss this play or relate it to "baddies" who carry guns as it would be inadvertently telling children that their parents are baddies! In many cases, weapon play can help bridge the gap between home and setting as many homes allow toys like nerf guns, crossbows and swords as part of fantasy play and dressing up. Educators can discuss safety and help children to manage appropriate levels of risk for themselves.

We do need to carefully think through how we allow gun play – for example, I personally would not allow replica guns in the role play area, but wouldn't mind if a child built one out of Lego. I would offer rules and boundaries and monitor the play to ensure that it was not violent, and try to scaffold the play to extend narratives and help it become more purposeful. Allowing children to play with guns enables us to have a conversation with them about what weapons are for and what they can do. In the same way that we might encourage children to use oven gloves with a toy oven and talk to the children about how things that are taken out of the oven are hot and we shouldn't touch them, we can also encourage our children to carry guns carefully in their play, for example, put them in a holster and keep the safety catch on and in real life never to touch a gun.

Ways that we can permit weapons appropriately include:

- Allowing children to use their imaginations to create guns or weapons.
- Offering loose parts and open-ended resources rather than "toy" guns and weapons.
- Joining in with their play and role modelling appropriate interactions.
- Discussing rules or codes of behaviour for weapon play, for example, only children who want to be involved can be "shot" at.
- Introducing safety aspects, for example, guns should be carried in holsters or swords are carried in sheaths.
- Introducing the idea of targets and using a sight to bring skill into aiming weapons.
- Showing YouTube clips of the Olympic shooting events or archery.
- Encouraging team games and cooperation.
- Fighting only imaginary baddies or monsters.
- Using goggles to protect eyes from foam bullets if playing with nerf or equivalent.
- Encouraging children to stage any fighting scenes in their play so that it becomes like an intricate dance and carefully choreographed routine – this requires a much higher level of skill.
- If playing war games, thinking about tactical planning and problem solving.
- As with other play, having high expectations about children's behaviour and establishing the rules of play.

In the USA, "Firearm-related deaths are the third leading cause of death overall among US children aged 1 to 17 years and the second leading cause of injury-related death" (Fowler et al., 2017). However, in the UK, although there has been a rise in the number of crimes involving knives or sharp instruments, there has been a decrease in the number of offences recorded by police which involve firearms (Office for National Statistics, 2018). In the UK, access to firearms by the general public is tightly controlled, which could partly or wholly account for these differences. I can honestly say that I don't know if my viewpoint would be different if I lived in a different country where guns were more readily available.

As children play they are exploring the world and often their toys of choice are miniature versions of adult tools. This was true of Afghan children who were choosing to play with toy and sometimes replica guns. The *Guardian* reported that, in 2015, Afghanistan banned toy guns in an effort to curb violent behaviour. It is too early to say whether this ban has resulted in less violent behaviour or not, however, it is a similar policy to that in Northern Ireland during the Troubles. This ban was also enforced due to the danger of playing out on the streets. The concern was that if children were playing with pretend or replica guns, adults with real guns might shoot first and find out it was a child with a replica later (and, sadly, this did happen).

We know that children regularly represent what they see in their lives through play and perhaps the majority of gun play seen in the UK would fall into fantasy play. In a different country it might be more readily described as sociodramatic play, which, based on their real-life experiences, has an important purpose in helping children to understand the adult world. My colleague Sue Martin lives in Canada where, despite being close geographically to the USA, there are tight gun laws more akin to those in the UK. When discussing the USA in relation to gun play she told me: "The children whose parents are incarcerated, those who are exposed to the greatest violence, those who have had adverse childhood experiences (ACEs) and toxic stress, are those who need the gun play the most. Saying 'no' to a child who is making a gun out of clay, Lego, cardboard or a stick, is probably not a good idea, but it is good to ensure that conversations are had about gun safety, and plenty of chats about "what do you think would happen if …' and 'how do you think someone feels if that gunshot hits them?'" Thus there is an opportunity within ECE to raise these issues, talk about the dangers of guns and reinforce the fact that in real life they are not toys.

In 2108, Erdman wrote an interesting article for the National Association for the Education of Young Children (NAEYC) in the USA about gun safety and supporting young children. She shares ideas about how to support youngsters to make informed decisions about guns if they potentially have access to the real thing and she uses her knowledge of child development to inform adults. For example, she talks about children being curious and keen to explore and therefore we cannot rely on hiding a gun away as a method of protecting children. The article is worth reading if you are in the position of having an actual gun that could be accessed by a child.

In the UK, knives and sharp instruments rather than guns are the weapon of choice for our violent criminals (Office for National Statistics, 2018). Obviously, we do not have replica knives in our settings, but we do (and should) allow children to use real knives as tools for cutting, whittling and spreading. We teach children what knives are for and how to use them safely. Surveys tell us that the main reason why adults might carry a weapon is under the misguided belief that it will protect them (Hasan, 2018) and that many of these weapons are then used against their owner, thus contributing to the culture of fear that exists in society today. The police in the UK warn against carrying a weapon and, according to the Home Office #knifefree campaign, statistics show that people who carry a weapon are more likely to be hospitalised with an injury caused by violence (2018). Thus we need to empower children to grow into adults who will not live in fear and who will stand firm against the violence they may encounter in society. Allowing weapon play gives us the opportunity to re-educate children about the dangers of weapons so that they can grow to be more responsible citizens in the future.

Weapon play does not have to be violent. Children can use various weapons to develop their skills and fine motor control.

One setting introduced targets and encouraged children to "fire" water pistols at the targets. On a different occasion, they asked the children to find V-shaped sticks and made catapults using a piece of elastic. They then created a "firing range" and placed plastic bottles on a tree stump and the children held a competition to see how many they could knock down.

In relation to weapon play (as opposed to playing with real guns), Chapter 7 explores how we can set boundaries and rules that will keep children safe and help to maintain a positive play atmosphere. For example:

- Only children (and adults) who are part of the play can shoot or be shot at.
- Pretend fights do not hurt others.
- No real hitting, prodding or stabbing with a weapon.
- You can leave or join the game at any time.
- Weapons should be carried safely and kept in holsters/carriers when not in use.
- Even toy guns should always have their safety catch on.
- The game should not upset anyone, if it does, the play must stop.

Does violent play lead to violent adults and more aggressive behaviour?

One concern raised when discussing aggressive and violent behaviour is about whether or not there is a correlation between playing with toy weapons and violence later in life. Thompson and Barker (2008) argue that there is no evidence that playing with guns in childhood causes adults to be more violent in nature. They suggest, however, that there is a gender link, because 60–80% of boys play with toys that could be deemed as aggressive in comparison with only around 30% of girls. They also associate this with children's feelings of power and dominance, as we see themes recurring around winning and losing, goodies and baddies, heroism and power. Chapter 4 considers gender in relation to superhero play in more detail.

Over the years there have been many studies that look at violence in childhood and how it relates to violence in adulthood. Some studies have found a link and others suggest there is no correlation. Thus the jury is still out. Sadly, there is clear evidence that children who have witnessed domestic violence or suffered abuse are more likely to become violent or abusive themselves or to become victims in adulthood (Unicef, 2006). One of the suggested therapies for such children is sociodramatic play when they can explore real-life events through play, therefore playing aggressively can also support children to understand what they have witnessed and experienced in a safe environment.

Behaviourism would suggest that children learn through imitating what they see and thus behave like other people. Bandura famously introduced the idea of children copying aggressive behaviour in his controversial "Bobo doll" experiment (1973). However, it must also be noted that the children in his experiments were using the doll in the way that it was designed to be used (hit, pushed etc.) and were copying a "more knowledgeable other" (MKO) and this observational learning diminishes as children grow older. Bandura also found that children watching aggressive behaviour on the television behaved more aggressively towards others. However, results from a recent study (Ferguson, 2015) suggest that media violence does not predict the increase in societal violence and scholars should be wary of stating that violent media viewing and participation always correlates with aggression. Having said that, in many families, the television is on in the background and therefore children may well be witnessing far more violence than we realise ... Could this be desensitising them and do children see it as the norm?

There are two sides to the debate, with some theorists in favour of allowing aggressive play because of the many noted benefits and others who suggest it should be prevented due to the risk of potentially increasing violent behaviour. Bergen (1994) argues that in the light of more violence in society, aggressive play sometimes teaches children to fear or destroy rather than celebrate difference and that it teaches that violence is a way of ending disputes. However, Braza et al. (2007) proposed that more aggressive play actually reduces aggression as it underlines the social hierarchies that children create in the playground and helps children to develop social intelligence. In addition, Harbin and Miller (1991, p. 80) argue that if we accept violent behaviours we can transform them into "constructive, developmental activities" and "violent behavior can be mediated into positive directions". They found in their research that four-year-old boys telling stories relating to an aggressive toy used more extensive language and were more communicative, which was seen as a positive response.

My own view is that playing aggressively is a natural urge for many children, particularly boys, and is observed within nature as many mammals engage in similar aggressive play. As early childhood educators, we should use this play as an opportunity to help children to understand about themes such as strength, dominance, power and social interaction. We also need to observe children more closely and recognise the differences between aggressive play and real violence and to *follow the children's lead.*

What does this mean in practice?

When I was growing up my sister and I often played cops and robbers and my husband remembers playing "cowboys and Indians". Some of these games are perhaps not appropriate to play today, but to a certain extent, superheroes are filling this void. Sometimes children can relate to the back stories of superheroes with some who are adopted, some orphaned and most from dysfunctional families. These backgrounds also help to grow the sense of shared culture. Children understand superhero play. It's predictable, there are goodies and baddies, it involves physical games such as running, chasing, rough and tumble and it's a very sociable experience. Characters change over time with popular culture but the themes remain the same: goodies, baddies, good, evil, death, killing and power. Good wins over evil.

Chapter 8 discusses more fully how we can manage this type of play in practice, however, some ideas include:

- Introduce rules for your superheroes and set limits and boundaries so that everyone knows where they stand.
- Have a word which stops the play. It could be "freeze" – in our home, it's actually "custard"! This enables you, or a child, to stop the play at any time and to check feelings.
- Teach children how to play safely and how to say no to others.
- Create an ethos of permission so that children are not faced with any false sense of "we're not allowed to …"
- Use puppets and soft toys to enable you to discuss aggression and violence, for example, introduce a puppet that was hurt in a play fight and talk to the children about how they could prevent this from happening again.
- Remind the children what a superhero would do in situ ...
- Ensure that you have covered this within your setting's policies – stand firm in your reasons for allowing (or not) more aggressive play.
- Write a risk assessment covering aggressive play.

- Provide action figures for small-world play "fight scenes".
- Offer open-ended resources e.g. loose parts, crates and den materials.
- Watch what you say – children may make a causal link – if you don't like my game and how I play, you don't like me.
- Beware of the "forbidden fruit" scenario – when something is banned it can often become more attractive! Banning this play can drive it underground with children lying or hiding their play to cover up their true intentions.
- Monitor and supervise their play without interfering too much.
- Observe closely and distinguish between play fighting and real aggression, intervening when appropriate.
- Introduce more male role models and support them when playing in physical ways with the children.
- Reframe how you think about more aggressive play – e.g. thinking in terms of heroic play may help you to become more accepting of it.

In summary

It is our duty to protect children from the darker forces of this world whenever possible and equip them to deal with their aggressive feelings and those of others. Sadly, however, many children have been exposed to various things that, given a choice, we would never wish them to be exposed to. We need to deal with the fallout of this exposure and support children to understand difficult concepts in a developmentally appropriate way.

Every early childhood setting is situated in a different context and it is important that early childhood educators decide for themselves where they will draw the line about aggressive play. It is my hope that I have opened up the discussion and clearly presented the benefits for children who engage in more aggressive play. We must be sensitive to the fact that when a type of play is deemed as negative or we try to stop children from playing in a certain way, this is sending messages to children that their imaginations and ideas are bad or that they are bad and can end up encouraging them to deceive us about their thoughts and feelings. Aggressive play can help children to understand themes relating to control, power, good and evil and provides educators the opportunity to raise difficult topics with young children.

Questions for reflection

1 What is your rationale for allowing or forbidding children to play games involving fighting, weapons and superheroes?
2 Do you have rules or boundaries about this type of play? If so, what are they?
3 Do you treat the interests of all children in the same way? For example, if a child is interested in guns do you allow him to pursue this interest during the session?
4 Are you giving boys the same opportunities to explore imaginative play as girls?

References

Bandura, A. (1973) *Aggression: A Social Learning Analysis*. Oxford, England: Prentice-Hall

Bergen, D. (1994) Should teachers permit or discourage violent play themes? *Childhood Education*, *70*(5), pp. 300ff

Bergnehr, D. and Cekaite, A. (2018) Adult-initiated touch and its functions at a Swedish preschool: controlling, affectionate, assisting and educative haptic conduct, *International Journal of Early Years Education*, *26*(3), pp. 312–331

Biben, M. and Suomi, S. (1993) Lessons from primate play in MacDonald, K. (Ed.) *Parent–Child Play: Descriptions and Implications*. Albany, NY: State University of New York Press

Braza, F., Braza, P., Carreras, R., Muñoz, M., Sánchez-Martín, R., Azurmendi, A.et al. (2007) Behavioral profiles of different types of social status in preschool children: an observational approach, *Social Behavior & Personality: An International Journal*, *35*(2), pp. 195–213

Cummings, E. M., Iannotti, R. J. and Zahn-Waxler, C. (1989) Aggression between peers in early childhood: individual continuity and developmental change, *Child Development*, *60*(4), pp. 887–895

Erdman, S. (2018) Viewpoint. Promoting gun safety: sharing knowledge of child development to support informed decisions, *Young Children*, *73*(1)

Ferguson, C. J. (2015) Does media violence predict societal violence? It depends on what you look at and when, *Journal of Communication*, *65*(1)

Fowler, K., Dahlberg, L., Haileyesus, T., Gutierrez, C. and Bacon, S. (2017) Childhood firearm injuries in the United States, *Pediatrics*, *140*(1)

Guardian (2015) Afghanistan bans toy guns to curb culture of violence. Retrieved from http://www.theguardian.com/world/2015/jul/22/afghanistan-bans-toy-guns-after-eid-al-fitr-injuries-to-curb-culture-of-violence

Harbin, J. and Miller, D. (1991) Violent play behaviour and language of four-year old boys: the significance of teacher mediation, *Early Child Development and Care*, *75*(1), pp. 79–86

Hasan, M. (2018) US gun owners are holding the country hostage – and I fear for my family's safety, *New Statesman*, 14 September, *147*(5436), p. 37

Holland, P. (2003) *We Don't Play with Guns Here. War, Weapon and Superhero Play in the Early Years*. Maidenhead: Open University Press
Home Office (2018) #Knifefree. Retrieved from https://www.knifefree.co.uk/know-the-risks/
Huber, M. (2017) *Embracing Rough-and-Tumble Play: Teaching with the Body in Mind*. St. Paul, MN: Redleaf Press
Hughes, B. (2012) *Evolutionary Playwork*. London: Routledge
Jarvis, P. and George, J. (2010) Thinking it through rough and tumble play. In Moyles, J. (Ed.) *Thinking about Play*. Maidenhead: Open University Press
Lindon, J. (2001) *Understanding Children's Play*. Cheltenham: Nelson Thorne
MacRae, C. (forthcoming 2019) The red blanket: a dance of animacy, *Global Studies of Childhood*
Manning, E. (2016) *The Minor Gesture*. London: Duke University Press
Office for National Statistics (2018) Crime in England and Wales: year ending June 2018. Retrieved from https://www.ons.gov.uk/peoplepopulationandcommunity/ crimeandjustice/bulletins/ crimeinenglandandwales/yearendingjune2018
Piper, H. and Smith, H. (2003) "Touch" in educational and child care settings: dilemmas and responses, *British Educational Research Journal*, *29*(6), pp. 879–894
Rich, D. (2003) Bang, bang! Gun play, and why children need it, *Early Education Journal*, Summer 2003. Retrieved from http://dianerich.co.uk/pdf/bang%20bang%20gun% 20play%20 and%20why%20children%20need%20it.pdf
Rosen, R. (2015) Children's violently themed play and adult imaginaries of childhood: a Bakhtinian analysis, *International Journal of Early Childhood*, *47*(2), pp. 235–250
Scott, E. and Panksepp, J. (2003) Rough-and-tumble play in human children, *Aggressive Behaviour*, *29*, pp. 539–551
Simon, A., Owen, C. and Hollingworth, K. (2016) Is the "quality" of preschool childcare, measured by the qualifications and pay of the childcare workforce, improving in Britain? *American Journal of Educational Research*, *4*(1), pp. 11–17
Spinka, M., Newberry, R. and Bekoff, M. (2001) Mammalian play: training for the unexpected, *Quarterly Review of Biology*, *76*(2), pp. 141–168
Thompson, M. and Barker, T. (2008) *It's a Boy. Your Son's Development from Birth to Age 18*. New York: Ballantine Books.
Tremblay, R. E. (2000) The development of aggressive behaviour during childhood: what have we learned in the past century? *International Journal of Behavioral Development*, *24*(2), pp. 129–141
Unicef (1989) United Nations Convention on the Rights of the Child. Retrieved from http:// www.unicef.org.uk/wp-content/uploads/2010/05/ UNCRC_PRESS200910 web.pdf
Unicef (2006) Behind closed doors. The impact of domestic violence on children. Retrieved from https://www.unicef.org/media/files/BehindClosedDoors.pdf

3 "I'm gonna kill you … you're dead!"

Dealing with notions of killing and death

Introduction

When my middle daughter was three and a half, she was playing in her room with her little sister, who was 22 months old at the time. I was in the spare room and heard: "Come here darling!" I said to myself: "Oh bless, how sweet!" and then heard, "Die! Die! Die!" I rushed in to find her trying to "kill" her little sister with a toy sword! Her target was obviously too far away, hence the sweet words! Thankfully, my little one was happily smiling and laughing at all the attention and the toy sword was not making contact with my youngest!

This type of play is fairly common, although it can sound shocking to us as adults. We must remember that this is fantasy play and the key is in these words: fantasy and play. They are not enacting what they want to happen; they are playing out a narrative in their imaginations. A few moments after my youngest was "killed" she was chasing after her big sister again and the play had moved on. This was not siblings at war (which does occasionally happen in our house!) or even a case of bullying; this was an innocent game in which two children were mutually playing together and exploring concepts difficult to understand.

Death and killing

Death is difficult for children to understand. It is an abstract idea and one that is hard even for many adults to grasp. Theorists consider the concept of death to be made up of five main components:

Inevitability – we will all die one day.

Universality – death applies to all living things.

Irreversibility – it is permanent.

Cessation – when we die our normal physical functions will cease.

Causality – it is a product of cause and effect. (Panagiotaki et al., 2018)

It is generally accepted that one of the purposes of children's play is to help them to understand the world around them and how it works, thus it should not be surprising that we will see all of these different components relating to death in children's play from time to time.

Children gradually understand more about the "deadness of dead" as they grow older. For example, according to child development theory (cited in Panagiotaki et al., 2018, p. 97): "Children as young as 5 years grasp the ideas that death is inevitable and irreversible, but most do not begin to understand universality and cessation until around 6 or 7 years" and children might not understand the causality component until they are nearly 10 years old. This fits with the idea that children learn in different ways and at different rates, making it difficult to generalise about their levels of understanding. It is generally accepted that the older the child, the better her understanding of death. In addition, an abstract topic such as death or killing may be better understood by a child who has had first-hand experience of a family member, friend or pet dying and less understood by a child who has only heard the terms on television. In the light of this, we cannot assume that young children fully grasp what words like "kill", "dead" and "die" mean and therefore we must not be concerned if children are using them in their play.

However, it could be argued that it's OK to allow children to play with themes relating to death, but killing is a whole different kettle of fish. Killing is about deliberately ending a life. One of the main ways that the concept of death is played with by children is through a narrative of killing and thus this theme needs to be acceptable in terms of their play because it offers us opportunities to discuss death with young children. Therefore, in my opinion killing and death are inextricably linked and cannot be separated from each other.

Case study – Preschool

Henry (four years two months) and Alex (three years 10 months) were "flying" around in the outside area, being "Superman". Their play quickly turned into unproductive, repetitive, chasing and they began running over children's games and spoiling their play, shouting "I'm gonna kill you" as they ran. Sarah, Henry's key person, asked the boys what they were doing. They said: "We're playing Superman and we're killing the baddies!" To which Sarah replied: "Oh, does Superman kill the baddies?" This led to a discussion about what the baddies had done (stolen some kryptonite and chased Superman) and how they could solve this as a problem. Sarah asked how Superman could track down the kryptonite and lock it away again. What followed was a complex storyline that involved Alex finding a bag to hide the kryptonite in and Henry banishing the baddie to another planet!

This scenario is regularly observed in early childhood settings throughout the United Kingdom and beyond. Henry and Alex are playing with the concepts of good versus evil, goodies and baddies and bringing killing into their play. Sarah observed their play and recognised that it could be more purposeful. She was also aware of the language of killing being used which she wanted to avoid. In most Superman stories, he takes the moral stance that killing is not the answer and will do everything he can to avoid killing his enemies; however, there are exceptional occasions when Superman has broken his own oath against killing. Sarah skilfully intervened, asking the boys questions that valued their play while, at the same time, extending the narrative and storyline.

It is worth noting that most superheroes fight evil and serve the purpose of good and it is usually on this level that we find the children interacting and role playing at superheroes. However, there are exceptions to this. Wonder Woman is a warrior princess and, as a warrior, she doesn't hesitate in tracking down enemies or killing them. Some children are experts on their heroes of choice. They will know the back stories better than we do and so we must be wary of making generalisations like: "All superheroes help people" or "Superheroes don't kill other people", without knowing the superhero we are talking about. Children love to correct us when we are wrong! You may find the tables in Appendices 2 and 3 helpful guides for knowing a little more about superheroes.

When we encounter children using words like "kill" or "die" and "dead" in their play, it would be good to further observe the play to ensure that it does not escalate into more violent play. You may choose to intervene to try to extend the play themes as Sarah did in the above case study. Nevertheless, you can use these themes as a way in to discussing these difficult topics. The previous chapter considered aggressive and violent behaviour and addressed the violent aspects of killing and this chapter will now go on to address children's understanding of death and dying.

The inevitability of death

I have heard it said that the only certainty in life is death. However, children do not readily understand this to be true. In fact, sometimes children can get upset and say something like "I don't want to die!" and a well-meaning parent could respond: "It's OK, it's just like going on a long trip ..." This response is not helpful and can even lead to misconceptions later in a child's life. When researching children under the age of three and their understanding of death and grief, Norris-Shortle, Young and Williams (1993) warn against using euphemisms to explain death to young children. For example, telling children that someone who has died has "gone on a journey", "God took them because they were so good" or they are now "sleeping peacefully" or "at rest" could lead to children misunderstanding death. They could wonder when the deceased will return from their trip, hate God for taking their loved one or decide to be bad so that God won't take them or simply feel worried about going to sleep at night, just in case they die. One practitioner shared with me about how a three-year-old child in their setting got really upset when going on holiday, because she had been told when her Nana died that Nana was "in the sky" ... When the little girl went on an aeroplane and looked out of the window, she had expected to see her Nana again and was devastated because she couldn't find her Nana in the sky.

To further complicate matters, in the superhero world, death is rarely the end of the story. Over the years many superheroes in films and comics have either died or nearly died and returned in another series, or even by the end of the film, stronger and ready to carry on the fight! In fact, there is even one superhero named *Resurrection Man*, whose main superpower is to do just this! In addition, some superheroes cannot die because they are immortal, which, in itself, offers us the opportunity to talk about what this means.

The universality of death

Within the human world, as opposed to the superhero one, every living thing will eventually die. This is a universal truth relating to death and one that children need to learn about in the same way that they need to learn that it is inevitable. Children are far more able to deal with death than we sometimes give them credit for. They will often surprise us with their resilience and matter-of-fact attitude. We need to talk openly and in a factual way about death, without trying to cover it up or hide it to protect children. Playing at superheroes offers children a chance to play with the universality of death in a safe context.

Death is as much a part of life as life itself. We must ensure that we allow children to talk about death and occasionally experience loss as this is part of our journey through this world. This ethos of permission will equip children when sad things happen and they will know how to respond when things do go wrong, people get ill or loved ones die. If children are always fully protected from these sadder parts of life, how will they grow up to cope with loss, grief and illness? An example of this is when I was walking to school with my daughters (who at the time were four, two and just under one year old). We came across a small mouse that was injured and was lying in the road. My eldest daughter was concerned that it would be hit by a car, so we used a large leaf to gently carry the mouse to the verge. On the way home from school, she looked for the mouse and, sadly, we found its dead body in the grass. As a parent, I had a choice. I could tell her that it was asleep or I could tell the truth that it had died. I chose to tell her the truth and she cried. As a Christian family, we then said a prayer for the mouse and I thanked God for all the wonderful creatures He had made. I hope that I made the right choice. Norris-Shortle et al. (1993) suggest that in assisting children to deal with death at a young age, we are helping them to deal with death in the future and giving them a healthier outlook on matters of life and death.

The irreversibility of death

In comics and superhero stories, death can be overruled; however, in the real world, it is irreversible. Perhaps we may be concerned that children don't fully understand the finality of death and that may be true, but unless the topic is discussed openly and in a developmentally appropriate way, our children will not have the opportunity to even think about it. They may struggle with the idea of change, endings and the forever aspects of death, but, then, don't we all? Death is permanent but, in children's games, it is temporary. Allowing people to die and come back to life in their play can enable educators to help children to understand the concept of permanence. We can reflect on this aspect of play with the children and compare it to real life. We need to ensure that our expectations do not inject a more adult view of death into their play. This will come with time.

Case study – preschool: playing dead

On one occasion when the children had "shot" adult M, she lay on the floor and played dead. This involved her lying very still and not moving for a long time. After a while the children wanted to investigate M but she continued to lie still even when she was prodded and probed! The children began to worry about M and eventually they wanted to shake her awake. This gave her the opportunity to explain to the children that she was pretending to be dead and if she really were dead, she would never have talked again, never have got up again and never been able to play with them again.

Object permanence begins as early as seven months old, when a child first realises that things exist even when she cannot see them. When I realise that mum exists even when I'm not with her, I am left with the worry of whether she will come back again if she leaves me. It is for this reason that often at around seven to nine months old we can observe a child, who had previously been happy to be left at nursery, suddenly become clingy and show separation anxiety. The concept of permanence will be explored by children for many years to come. Just as Kohlberg (1966) suggests that children do not understand gender permanence until about seven years old, I believe that children do not understand the permanence of death until around this age either. The struggles that children have with the idea of permanence is evident through their play and experiences, for example, they regularly play hiding games, dislike parents leaving or find it difficult to say goodbye after a play date or stay at Grandma's …

When she was five my youngest child didn't want me to go to work and clung desperately to my leg. She said: "If you go I'll die of miss-vation!" I asked what miss-vation was and she replied: "It's like starvation only because I'll miss you so much!" In this example, she is playing with the concept of death and missing people and relating the two. Even now at age seven, she often asks me: "Will you think of me when you're at work?" and "Will I miss you when I'm at school?" Attachment theory and building secure attachments within early childhood contribute to a child's positive health and wellbeing in later life. We can help children by being more aware of attachment issues and how they affect young children. Bath Spa University has worked with a number of schools within Bath and North East Somerset Local Authority looking at ways in which they can become more attachment aware. I believe that we can use these ideas to ensure that early childhood educators are also more aware of attachment issues.

Attachment aware educators need to:

- Be child centred and acknowledge children's different attachment styles.
- Create nurturing relationships to promote children's learning and behaviour and satisfy children's innate need to have a secure "sense of belonging".

- Acknowledge adults' roles as a potential secondary attachment figure that can help to reshape insecure attachment behaviours and support the development of more secure ones.
- Create appropriate nurturing infrastructures for children with emotional and behavioural impairments (as they do for physical and learning impairments).

(adapted from Parker, Rose and Gilbert, 2016, p. 471)

Goodbyes are difficult – through the eyes of a child – will I ever see them again? Time is meaningless when you do not yet understand the difference between a second, a minute, an hour, a day, a month, a year ... If you imagine a three-year-old, a year is actually one-third of their lifetime! Imagine someone trying to talk to you about forever! This is not just a year or two, but many more years than you have been alive! It starts to blow your mind a little ...

We can help children to understand the concept of time by talking in terms of things that they know about for example, meals or sleeps. "You will go to Grandma's again in six sleeps" Or "We'll meet up with your friend after lunch, so one more meal ..." The other thing we can do to support children is to use a visual timetable. This can help children to follow our routine in a pictorial way.

Lunch time

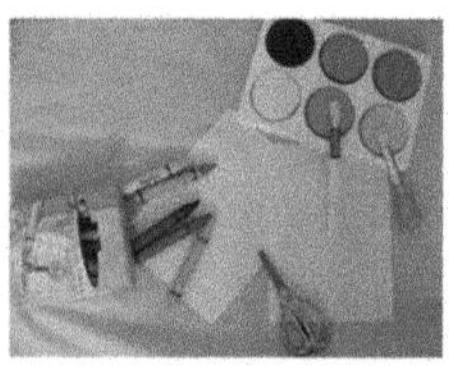

Activity time

Story time

Home time

With regard to death, we can talk to children in terms of memories. I really liked the way that a colleague talked to her daughter about things when her dog, Zuri, died. She understood that young children are unable to focus on too many ideas at once and that they find abstract thinking difficult, therefore she used the principle of three things and stated three truths about the dog:

1. Zuri had cancer.
2. The cancer made her heart stop.
3. She's not coming back but we always have our lovely memories of her.

In sharing these three things, she was able to talk factually with her daughter while, at the same time, explaining the irreversibility of death. After my father died, my youngest child asked when she was going to see him again, despite my explaining that he wouldn't

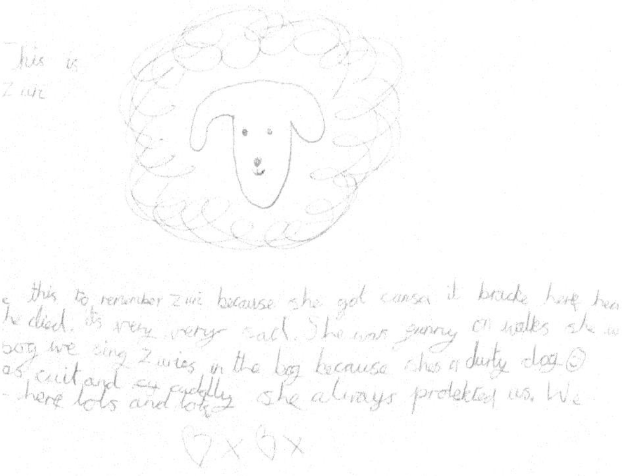

be coming back. We must accept these and other blunt comments from children as they grapple with understanding the permanence of death. They do not have a concept of forever and we shouldn't expect them to grieve in the same way as an adult. Sometimes questioning life and death and playing with the concepts are part of their process of understanding.

The cessation of our lives in death

It can be easier to talk to children about death in terms of concrete things (Hoffman and Strauss, 1985), like my colleague did above when she explained that the dog's heart stopped. So saying that someone who is dead can no longer move or breathe or will not visit our house again would be a good place to start. "At this age, death means no eating, no sleeping, and no playing" (Norris-Shortle et al., 1993, p. 739). Relating death to biological properties makes it more concrete and enables children to understand the difference between living and non-living. For example, to decide if something is alive we can talk to children about them eating, breathing and having babies. Therefore in this example we can talk to children about death in terms of their not eating, breathing or having babies any more (Slaughter, 2005). In the playing dead case study above, educator M linked the permanence of death to not talking, not getting up and not being able to play with them, all concepts that help children to understand the cessation of our lives in death.

It is important to accept all questions that children ask relating to death and dying and try to answer them honestly. It is better to be upfront and fully explain things to young children rather than sweeten the pill and try to skirt around the issues. Another example of a child misunderstanding the cessation of our lives in death was shared by a practitioner whose key child had been told that his deceased grandparent was "watching over him". This caused lots of problems for the child as he stopped wanting to go to the toilet because he didn't want Granny watching him. Children perceive "watching over" to mean within sight so this gave him mixed messages about what being dead actually means.

Kübler-Ross (1969), who famously conceived the five stages of grief, used the analogy of a cocoon and butterfly when supporting young children with death. She sees the cessation of the caterpillar's life and the new life of the butterfly as a visual example for young children and one which they can relate to. Stickney (1982) uses a similar story about waterbeetles and dragonflies to explain death to young children. She extends this idea to also explain why someone who has died is unable to come back again because the waterbeetle had a new body, with shining wings that wouldn't allow him to go back underwater. Children can often grasp the most profound and complex ideas very easily when shared within a story that they can connect with.

In researching this chapter, I read an interesting article in which the authors found that: "The topic of death is not unfamiliar to most children, despite some caregivers' predictions" that implied otherwise (Gaab, Owens and MacLeod, 2013). From their research, they found that five to seven-year-old children actually understood more than parents and carers thought they would when discussing death. They concluded that we must not shelter children from the topic of death and should remain honest with children about issues relating to death. In addition, we can role model cessation of life during superhero play, for example, if you are "killed" during play, you could fall to the ground and demonstrate that you are no longer able to walk and talk and need to exit the game. Children love it when you join in with their play and one practitioner found that the children didn't want to "kill" her because they wanted her to remain part of the plot!

It is worth noting, perhaps unsurprisingly, that additional research has shown that parents' religious beliefs regarding afterlife will influence, to an extent, children's beliefs and understanding of death (Panagiotaki et al., 2018). Therefore we need to be conscious of our beliefs and how they match or differ from those of the families we are serving to ensure that we remain respectful and do not further confuse our children with different interpretations relating to death.

The causality of death

The last component of death is about its causality, or the fact that, in death, our bodies break down and cease to work as they should. Children often think about causality in terms of plants and the changes in nature during the seasons, however, thinking about it in terms of death is more abstract. We need to be careful if we tell the children that a person died because they are old or because they were very sick. Children often make generalisations and assumptions from our statements as I found to my horror when one of my children asked her paternal grandfather how old he was. He answered "very old" to which she replied: "Well, why aren't you dead then!"

Norris-Shortle et al. (1993, p. 739) suggest that we listen to children's questions and what they say and spend time reassuring our children that just because we are getting older doesn't mean we are going to die soon, saying something like: "I am planning to be here a long time and help you grow up." We can help children to understand that bodies can break down by looking at nature and considering how the seasons change and how a leaf can fall and become compost for another leaf to grow in. One setting used a decaying leaf to encourage discussions about the cycle of life, growth, death and decay.

Case study – childminder

Our Muddy Footprints is a childminding team that is spurred on by the ever-enclosing environments our children are growing used to and the possibility of nature deficit disorder (Louv, 2005). To counteract this they actively make regular trips to their local nature spots to allow children unstructured time there. They visit locations that are as natural as possible such as woods, beaches and open commons. These sessions allow children the opportunities to see changes within the environment and decay first hand. During one outside session, a child found a tiny leaf that magically encapsulated all of the colours of decay. This tiny leaf sparked discussions about how leaves decompose and the cycle of life and death.

Children might also use the principle of cause and effect to draw an incorrect conclusion that, in some way, they have caused someone's death. Thus it is really important to reassure the child that they haven't caused the death and they are not the reason why everyone is sad. Being genuinely honest with children is always the best policy when it comes to sharing about death. We talk about encouraging children to be more emotionally literate and a key way to support children to understand their emotions is to acknowledge and label them. When you are sad, tell the children you feel sad. When you are angry explain that you feel angry. Children need to understand that having these feelings is part of being human and it's OK. However, we must realise that when we have these intense feelings, how we respond may not be OK. For example, it's OK to feel envious of my friend's new toy but when I feel that way it is not OK to take my friend's toy. These ideas fit within an emotion coaching approach.

Based on the work of John Gottman (Gottman, Katz and Hooven, 2013), emotion coaching focuses on supporting children in their emotional development and acknowledging their feelings. It recognises that all emotions are valid and acceptable, yet some ways that our emotions may lead us to behave are not. For example, it's okay to feel angry, but it's not okay to throw a chair when you feel angry. We can also use emotion coaching to help children to come to terms with something like the death of a pet.

Emotion coaching in practice

STEP 1: Recognising feelings, empathising, validating the feelings and labelling them.

STEP 2: Explore the issue/setting limits on behaviour where necessary.

STEP 3: Problem solving with the child and finding a way forward.

Sometimes as adults we are dismissive of children's emotions and their emotional response without meaning to be. For example, if a child is upset about the death of a pet, we may try to soothe them, saying "Don't cry!" or offering to buy them a new pet. These responses may not help the child at the time. If we use an emotion coaching approach, we would say: "What a shock that your pet Bertie has died, you must feel very sad. He was a good friend to you. You really enjoyed playing together didn't you?" You could then go on to talk about your happy memories about the pet and perhaps try to make a photo book all about Bertie. This approach doesn't offer false hope, pretend that Bertie hasn't died or brush over that he has died, instead, it faces the facts, demonstrates empathy and acknowledges and labels the child's feelings while finding a positive way forward.

Experiences such as losing a pet can be helpful preparatory experiences for children and may really help them when they experience human loss of a close personal friend or family member for the first time. Children often show a keen interest in dead animals, such as a dead insect or fly. Discussing death as part of lifecycles is a useful way of approaching the topic with young children. The case study below from Odstock Day Nursery outlines how one setting approached the topic when a dead baby bird was found.

Case study – Odstock Day Nursery

Odstock Day Nursery is situated in an old Victorian schoolhouse in a rural village near Salisbury. It includes work on lifecycles as part of the core planning for all age groups within the nursery. House martins regularly nest in the eaves of the house and sometimes young fall from their nests. On one occasion, some three-year-old children found a dead chick lying on the floor. One child, Sally, insisted that it was asleep. Another child, Charlie, said it was hurt. Sally agreed that it might be hurt but it was still sleeping. Charlie said if it was hurt and asleep we need to find its mum because mums help babies. They looked up at the nest but could only see more babies sticking their beaks out and cheeping.

A practitioner asked: "Do you think it's asleep? I'm not sure ..."

The children discussed why it would have its eyes shut if it weren't asleep, then they gently poked the bird. It didn't move. They thought it might be dead. The practitioner asked the children to feel their hearts beating and then feel for the bird's heartbeat. They couldn't find a heartbeat.

On realising that it was dead, the children discussed what to do with the bird. They wanted to protect it so they wrapped it in paper towels and put it in a box. Sally wanted to show her dad when he arrived to collect her.

The practitioner made sure that she primed Sally's dad before he collected Sally so that he was able to respond positively.

The children were very gentle and tentative when showing Sally's dad the bird. They looked at the wing, eyes and beak with interest. Sally's dad asked the children where it had come from and they told him it had fallen from the nest.

The children were not upset and were very matter of fact about it all. This experience was totally led by the children and very sensitively dealt with by the practitioner who gently scaffolded their conversation throughout. For many children, this was the first time they had come into contact with a dead animal and it was a very positive experience.

Coping with family bereavement

Sadly, there may be children in our settings who lose a loved one. Perhaps their parent or grandparent dies while the children are in our care. We need to ensure that we offer plenty of opportunities for the child to talk about how they feel and liaise closely with the family over how they are dealing with the loss. Some families will talk of heaven or being in a "happier place", while other families would not want to entertain such talk. Therefore it is vital that we understand and respect their wishes. What we can do is offer a space in which to talk about their feelings if they want to. For example, when my friend lost her baby, her daughter spent some time playing at our house. Initially, I wasn't sure whether to talk about her baby brother or not, but she wanted to talk about him. We then painted a picture for her brother and on another occasion made a model for her to take home to her mummy. While we were painting we were free to talk about how sad we felt about her brother and how it's okay to feel sad sometimes. Our time together was a special sharing time and, I hope, helped her, albeit in a small way, to deal with her baby brother's death.

There are many groups and charities that can offer advice and support if you are helping a child to deal with bereavement and loss. It is always a good idea to seek additional advice. There are also lots of books and supporting materials available.

Key principles when supporting children with bereavement:

- Be as honest as possible with the child and use terms that are factual and portray information, avoiding the potential for misunderstandings.
- Remember that a bereavement brings children a lot of uncertainty, so try to ensure that changes in your setting are kept to a minimum. Familiar surroundings can help a child to remain feeling safe and secure.
- Reassure children that they are still loved and protected.
- Never be offended or affronted by the directness of a young child's questions and comments. They are trying to fathom the unfathomable and we need to remain sensitive to their needs, even if they appear to be insensitive themselves.
- Answer any questions that the child has to the best of your ability, being genuine and honest in your answers. Don't worry if a child asks the same questions over and over again. They are trying to reassure themselves and we must answer consistently each time as this will offer the reassurance they are seeking.
- If they don't want to talk, don't make them. Give them time to process what has happened but ensure that they know you are there if they need you.
- Children's behaviour may regress after a bereavement, for example, by wetting themselves, thumb sucking or becoming excessively clingy to a carer. We must offer understanding, reassurance and security at this time and not chastise these behaviours. They will pass with time as the child feels more safe and secure.
- Invest in some resources and stories that aim to support children and families with bereavement.
- Explain to children how you feel and why, for example, I am crying because I am sad. I am sad because Granddad has died and I won't see him again.
- Family rituals around death should be explained to children and, whenever possible, children should be given the choice about attending services of remembrance, funerals, burials and cremations.
- We can enable children to engage in rituals that will support the grieving process, for example, lighting a candle or looking at photographs and reminiscing about the person who has died.

What does this mean in practice?

It is important that we offer children the opportunity to play with the idea of death and killing and are accepting if these themes overlap into their play. Lots of Disney stories begin with the death of a parent or loss of a loved one and many children are familiar with these stories and therefore (whatever your personal view of such stories) they can be a useful resource to use. However, beware of the fast-forwarding effect … I knew a young person who told me that their parent had always fast-forwarded the beginning of *Finding Nemo* when Nemo's mother dies … several years later, they were devastated to find out the truth! My children struggle with anxiety and we have to be careful about what they watch on television, so we are guilty of a similar level of protection, fast-forwarding the scary or sad bits … So always check with parents if you are using multimedia or video clips in your setting.

Some ideas of how to appropriately support children in thinking about death include:

- Have an ethos of permission within the setting so that words like "kill", "dead" and "die" are not banned from your vocabulary but instead prompt discussion.
- Use superhero play as an opportunity to engage in discussions that explore the concept of death.
- Engage in sociodramatic play in which children role play events from their lives.
- Read stories and books that include death or deal with bereavement and grief.
- Storytelling – making up stories in which a character dies or undergoes changes.
- Provide opportunities for children to make up their own stories (e.g. helicopter stories).
- Use puppets and role play to prompt discussion.
- Introduce children to the idea of lifecycles, for example, butterflies.
- Raise some chicks from eggs, butterflies from caterpillars or look after a class/setting pet.
- Think about changes over time in the natural world, e.g. growth and decay.
- Share some memories about a special person you know who has died and reminisce about the good times you shared together.
- Answer any questions about death as honestly as possible remembering that it's OK to say "I don't know!"
- Use correct language: dead, death, dying, died, buried etc.

In summary

In the past, as recently as only 100 years ago, children were not protected from death and dying in the way that modern children can be, because death was part of the families' home life. Ill and dying people were nursed at home, some children died young, many adults died at a younger age than nowadays. Mortality rates looking at age of death have steadily decreased due to many reasons such as improved medicine and healthcare. I don't know if death was talked about more than it is today, but I can assume that children had more first-hand experience of death and dying. We need to ensure that we open up a dialogue with children about death and dying and talk to them in developmentally appropriate ways to help them to gain an understanding of these issues. As early childhood educators, we have a responsibility to support children to understand these complex issues and to recognise death as the final part of the lifecycle, in order for them to grow into well-adjusted adults who can cope with bereavement.

Questions for reflection

1. How do you currently respond to children who use phrases involving killing and death?
2. Are there any ways in which you can further support children to understand about death as a part of life?
3. Can you see any opportunities to use an emotion coaching approach in your setting?

References

Gaab, E. M., Owens, G. R. and MacLeod, R. D. (2013) Caregivers' estimations of their children's perceptions of death as a biological concept, *Death Studies*, *37*(8), pp. 693–703

Gottman, J., Katz, L. and Hooven, C. (2013) *Meta-Emotion: How Families Communicate Emotionally*. Abingdon: Routledge.

Hoffman, S. and Strauss, S. (1985) The development of children's concepts of death, *Death Studies*, *9*(5–6), pp. 469–482

Kohlberg, L. (1966) A cognitive-developmental analysis of children's sex-role concepts and attitudes. In Maecoby, E. E. (Ed.) *The Development of Sex Differences.* Stanford, CA: Stanford University Press

Kübler-Ross, E. (1969) *On Death and Dying.* New York: Macmillan.

Louv, R. (2005) *Last Child in the Woods: Saving Our Children from Nature-Deficit Disorder.* Chapel Hill, NC: Algonquin Books

Norris-Shortle, C., Young, P. A. and Williams, M. A. (1993) Understanding death and grief for children three and younger, *Social Work*, *38*(6), pp. 736–742

Panagiotaki, G., Hopkins, M., Nobes, G., Ward, E. and Griffiths, D. (2018) Children's and adults' understanding of death: cognitive, parental, and experiential influences, *Journal of Experimental Child Psychology*, *166*, 96

Parker, R., Rose, J. and Gilbert, L. (2016) Attachment aware schools: an alternative to behaviourism in supporting children's behaviour? In Lees, H. and Noddings, N. (Eds.) *Palgrave International Handbook of Alternative Education*. London: Palgrave Macmillan.

Slaughter, V. (2005) Young children's understanding of death, *Australian Psychologist*, *40*(3), pp. 179–186

Stickney, D. (1982) *Waterbugs and dragonflies – explaining death to children*. Boston, MA: Pilgrim Press.

4 "Boys will be boys!"

Considering gender in relation to superhero play

Introduction

We all know boys who are sensitive and good writers and we know girls who like nothing better than to kick about with a football or to dress as Spider-Man. But being masculine and feminine is not about which sex you are born as, it is about gender, which is a concept steeped in culture and strong opinions. Therefore, when we consider gender in relation to superhero play, we begin unpicking some huge issues. Are both boys are girls engaging in superhero play in our settings? What messages does this type of play give our children in relation to gender, overtly or covertly? How can we ensure a balance between competent, strong girl superheroes as well as the damsel in distress and how can we be sensitive to children's needs as their understanding of gender develops?

Children appear to enjoy deconstructing polar opposites such as good and evil, death and life and also enjoy unpicking gender roles in terms of what would be considered male and female. Superhero play is the perfect opportunity to incorporate these ideas and explore these extremes and even to blur the lines a little. This play involves power and powerlessness, control and chaos and can enable our children to unpick what is meant by these ideas.

Nature or nurture?

During courses, I often ask practitioners to imagine a line across the room with nature at one end and nurture at the other end. I invite them to go and stand on the line at a place that represents their understanding. Is gender innate and something you're born with, so purely a question of nature or is gender totally dependent on the experiences and the environment that the child grows up in and therefore a question of nurture?

As you can imagine, many practitioners sit on the fence on this – stating that both nature and nurture are hugely influential when it comes to gender and I'm inclined to agree. We know that we are born with specific chromosomes, reproductive organs and hormones, meaning that there are biological differences between males and females, however, we also know that the environment hugely influences children as they learn and develop. So, in my mind, gender has to be influenced by both nature and nurture, what proportion of each I'm not sure. Sex describes whether we are born male or female in terms of our biological makeup and gender refers to the cultural differences expected of men and women according to their sex, which is usually seen as more of a continuum now, thus men can have feminine traits and women masculine ones, while others still prefer not to identify with either and would be described as non-binary.

However, it could be argued that we cannot simplify our understanding of gender to nature and nurture as our understanding also develops as a result of our own self-efficacy and self-development as children work out a sense of identity for themselves. So perhaps worrying about nature and nurture is a red herring and we should instead ensure that our attention remains firmly on the child herself. Let's first consider how children's understanding of gender develops.

Mars and Venus!

Clearly there are biological differences between males and females and it is possible to make generalisations according to gender. It is generally accepted that boys develop physically, emotionally, socially and cognitively later than girls and that they respond and react to stimuli in ways different from those of girls. For example, boys are more likely to engage in rough and tumble play or play more aggressively than girls (Thompson and Barker, 2008). We need to be aware of these differences while remaining wary of turning these generalisations into prejudice and therefore thinking that all boys do x, y, z or all girls like a, b, c … A stereotype is when we hold beliefs about different people because of a characteristic, in this case, gender, and although they are a way of organising thinking and not automatically negative, we need to be wary of stereotyping. This is because stereotypes are closely linked with prejudice and discrimination and we need to ensure that our beliefs about boys and girls do not result in negative behaviour, thoughts or anyone being acted against unfairly or unjustly.

Another area where boys and girls differ is in terms of language and communication. Boys tend to develop language more slowly than girls, which has led many studies to consider how educators engage boys in language and literacy programmes. Wilson (2006) identified that girls use 10 to 30 times more language in their play and there are various barriers to boys' learning, including a lack of independence and, significantly, a lack of emotional development stemming from poorer language skills.

These poorer skills are also apparent when we look at academic achievement. In the UK, the Early Years Foundation Stage Profile measures children's achievement against standard Early Learning Goals at age five and girls perform better than boys in all key measures, including reading and writing (DfE, 2018). Although narrowing, the gap between the achievement of boys and girls continues to be evident throughout primary school particularly when considering aspects related to literacy. Educators regularly discuss strategies to support boys and address this underachievement and it is my view that superheroes can be a great source of inspiration that boys will want to read and write about.

It has been noted that there are also hundreds of differences in male and female brains and it is a popular misconception that there are male and female brains. However, we must remain cautious not to focus on these differences because as a professor from Tel Aviv University found there were more similarities than differences between the sexes in terms of their brains (Joel et al., 2018). Thus a more measured approach might be to talk about children in terms of their likes and dislikes or their interests and not focus on gender at all.

Bayley and Featherstone stated: "Each individual boy and girl has different needs, behaviours and strengths. Recognising these and working to meet them will help us to ensure that every child is treated as the unique being they are, and that with real equality of opportunity to access individualised support, they can achieve their potential" (2010, p. 5). If we begin with the child and their interests and fascinations, their gender does not need to come into it. So we must find out about our children and use what we know about them to support their learning, regardless of whether they are girls or boys. If they show an interest in superhero play, we can use this theme to engage both boys and girls.

The development of children's understanding relating to gender

Babies are not born with a full understanding of gender and the cultural expectations relating to it that develop over time. Children recognise that there are differences between males and females and research has shown that babies can distinguish between male and female voices and faces and that this is linked to social interaction (Richoz et al., 2017). Toddlers are able to label themselves according to their gender and by around two years old, children are beginning to use gender labels for others and repeat phrases or attitudes related to gender that are shown at home, for example: "Big boys don't cry!"

By around three years old children begin to notice gender and physical differences between themselves and others, however they are still working out a sense of self and may be easily influenced by societal norms and biases, for example, they may adopt the idea that pink is for girls and blue is for boys. By the time children are about four or five years old they can often be seen engaging in gender appropriate play as defined by social norms, for example, boys might play with trains and cars and girls might play with dolls and enjoy colouring. Sometimes at this age, we hear children refusing to play with others and using gender as the reason why they don't want to play, for example, a girl might say that a boy cannot play in the home corner because boys are not allowed. However, even at this age, children do not have a full understanding of gender and gender differences. As children grow and spend more time outside their home, they become more influenced by others, for example, friends, teachers and things that they watch on TV or games they play. So children's understanding of gender tends to be socially constructed and based on the experiences of the child.

In the past research often found that young children have definite ideas of gender roles within the home, however, recent changes within society mean that fewer adults are adhering to these roles. For example, fathers are often also very "hands-on" in terms of caregiving, changing nappies or bottle feeding their children and mothers regularly return to work and do not stay home as the sole caregiver, cooking, cleaning and looking after children. There are now fewer gender roles within professions, with both men and women becoming doctors, nurses, soldiers and bank managers. These small changes in society have also influenced how our young children think about gender with fewer stereotypical roles being recognised. In addition, within ECE we are careful to challenge stereotypical views and settings now ensure that our books and resources do not reinforce gender stereotypes.

When thinking about gender, Kohlberg is one of the key theorists who comes to mind. He came up with a developmental theory that suggests that children's understanding of gender develops with age (Kohlberg, 1966; see also Table 4.1). The first stage, gender labelling, occurs by the age of around three when children can label themselves and others accurately according to gender. A year or two later children in the gender stability stage can appreciate that this gender classification remains constant over time, for example, that a boy grows up to be a man. However, it is not until around six or seven years of age when children enter Kohlberg's final stage, gender consistency or gender permanence, where children realise that gender remains consistent and is not linked to time, context or physical features. Others have built on this theory suggesting that a full understanding of gender permanence, which takes into account genitals, does not develop until nearer nine years of age (McConaghy, 1979). So by about eight years old a child would probably realise that if I were to cut my hair short and wear my husband's clothes, I would remain a woman, despite appearances. A younger child might not be sure or may even say that I had changed into a man. Therefore, within ECE, the children we are working with do not have a full understanding of the permanence of gender, they are developing their own sense of gender identity and working out that of others, mainly using behavioural and visual cues.

Table 4.1 Kohlberg's stages of gender development

Stage	*Approximate age range*	*Description*
Stage 1: Gender labelling	Up to 3 years	Children can identify themselves and other people as girls or boys (mummies or daddies). However, gender is not seen as stable over time or across changes in superficial physical characteristics (e.g. length of hair, clothes)
Stage 2: Gender stability	4–5 years	Children recognise that gender is stable over time: boys will grow up to be men and girls will grow up to be women However, the unchanging nature of gender – that it remains the same regardless of changes in superficial appearance or activity choice – is not yet appreciated
Stage 3: Gender consistency	Over 6 or 7	Children have a full appreciation of the permanence of gender over time and across situations

(Adapted from Banerjee, 2005, p. 159)

Challenging gender stereotypes and addressing discrimination

Occasionally we will come across attitudes and views that are contrary to ours. It is vital that, if we encounter discriminatory or derogatory comments or actions, we challenge these giving reasons as to why we disagree. This is particularly important within the early years, because, as we have noted, children are still working out what it means to be male and female and are easily shaped and influenced by the views and attitudes of other people.

Daniel is three and a half and loves to engage with role play. When he arrives he goes straight to the dressing-up chest and chooses who he will be that day … He also enjoys using props with his play and will often be seen with a superhero mask, carrying a baby or wielding a pirate cutlass! Last week his father came to drop him off for a change and briefly stayed while Daniel settled in. Daniel choose to wear a fairy princess costume on this particular day and his father was horrified and insisted that Daniel take it off. He told the practitioners that under no circumstances was Daniel allowed to dress like a girl or play with girl's toys as he did not want him to be labelled as gay.

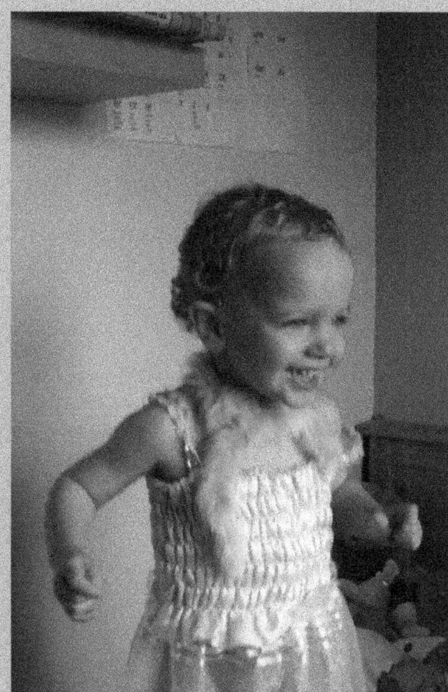

Daniel's key person, Sarah, decided to address this with Daniel's father and asked to have a quick word with him. They openly talked about Daniel and his love of imaginative play. Sarah asked if Daniel's father remembers using his imagination when he was growing up. Did he turn out to be the person that he dressed up as? Sarah explained that children love to pretend and play imaginative games and that dressing in a dress would not in any way make Daniel more feminine in the same way that wielding a cutlass would not actually make him a pirate. She shared that she felt uncomfortable with the way that he had talked about labelling people as gay because this sounded derogatory and discriminatory. She also shared the messages that their setting try to promote, outlined clearly within their policies, that toys are not gendered and children are free to play with any that they find inviting. Daniel's father was a little embarrassed in having this conversation and insisted that he hadn't meant anything bad by his comments. He agreed that Daniel was obviously enjoying using his imagination and agreed that he had overreacted.

The setting that Daniel attended had a clear inclusion and equalities policy that they were able to refer the father to, explaining that all children were welcome to "pretend" play at anything. In addition, the setting was able to reassure Daniel's father by showing him photographs of Daniel playing in more gender neutral or more typically "male" ways, while reiterating that dressing in pink or playing with "girls' toys" will not label him as gay or affect his sexuality in any way. The setting also decided to make a booklet aimed at parents explaining the benefits of dressing up and pretending. They gave this to all parents at the nursery.

As I discuss gender with early childhood settings, it is clear that the attitude that this father demonstrated is still rife and a common viewpoint that settings need to challenge. As the Stonewall guidance document *Getting Started* suggests, the consequences of not challenging stereotypes are significant. They estimate that 20,000 children are growing up in families with same-sex parents and there are many more with LGBT family and friends (2017). Therefore when we come across attitudes like this that are discriminatory we have a duty to speak out and help to prevent prejudice as children grow up.

Case study – preschool

While monitoring the use of their outside play area, one setting noticed that more boys were climbing than girls. During one observation they heard some four–year-old children while they are climbing on a low branch of a tree.

Tom: "This tree is only for boys isn't it?"

Peter: "Yes 'coz boys can climb and girls can't."

Sally: "I'm a good climber; at the park I got to the top of the web."

Tom: "But not this tree – this is for boys!"

Sally: "I can climb it higher, higher, higher!" She starts to climb onto the branch but Tom is in the way.

Peter: "No, girls can't climb trees!"

Sally goes round to the other side and starts to climb there away from Peter and Tom.

After monitoring their outside area and completing this observation, the practitioners met to discuss how to address their concerns. They came up with an action plan to combat this exclusive behaviour and to challenge the viewpoints that had been aired. Over time the boys and girls both climbed trees in the setting and the practitioners were able to challenge some of the views held relating to gender and equality.

The key strategies that the setting adopted in order to challenge this stereotype included:

- Explaining to the children that both boys and girls can climb trees.
- Using stories such as *This is Our House* (Rosen, 2007) to address the idea of exclusivity.
- Creating a scenario whereby the class teddy was excluded from playing on the bikes because the toy monkey had said that bears can't ride bikes because they are bears. They then talked to the children about how the teddy felt and why they thought the monkey said this. Was this true and fair?
- Finding examples of women who were tree surgeons and climbers and sharing pictures and stories with the children.
- One female practitioner role modelling climbing the tree.
- Encouraging the children to climb together on the same part of the tree.

Part of our role as an early childhood educator is to challenge if we hear derogatory marks or encounter discrimination of any kind in our settings, whether by a parent or a child. Ignoring it is condoning and accepting the remarks. This can be difficult. Here are some ideas which may help you:

- *Ensure that your policy is clear and referred to* as this gives you a foundation on which to rely. It can also help to work in partnership with parents and carers so that everyone is clear about the ethos.
- *Actively listen to what is being said and then show the other person that you understand them.* In this way, you demonstrate understanding for their point of view, even if you don't agree with it.
- *Ask for further clarification before you jump in!* For example, probe with questions such as: "What do you mean by that?" "Can you explain your viewpoint in a bit more detail?" It may simply be a misunderstanding.
- *Say what you think and what you feel.* This enables you to directly state your thoughts or feelings without apology. Own your feelings by making "I" statements, for example: "I feel uncomfortable when girls are referred to as the weaker sex because both girls and boys can be powerful and strong."
- *Focus on the behaviour not the person.* For example, instead of saying "You are sexist", say "'The remark you made was sexist."
- *Explain clearly why the remarks made were wrong or hurtful talking about the feelings of all involved.* This helps others to empathise and understand what is right and wrong and why.

- *Be specific; don't generalise.* For example, instead of saying "Remarks like that are stereotyping" you could say: "Boys will be boys is a stereotype and we need to make sure that we are presenting boys in a less stereotypical way."
- *Say what you want to happen.* This is very important so that you say in a clear and straightforward way what action or outcome you want without hesitancy, apology or aggression. For example "Please don't refer to boys in this way."
- *Earn the right to challenge others by being open to challenge yourself.* It is easy to use common phrases without thinking about the messages they are giving. We all need to reflect on our practice and have open discussions with others about what we mean.
- *Remember to act as a role model.* Behave in the way you would like others to behave and talk in the way that you expect to be spoken to.
- *Think about the reason why you are challenging.* This will enable you to clarify your point of view. For example, explain to the parent concerned about their little boy playing with the pram that it is important for children to develop their imaginative play skills and that plenty of fathers push prams and buggies – he is copying what he has seen in society.

As an educator, I wish I had been given a pound for every time I heard comments like this: "Boys, line up at the door. ...", "Girls wash your hands first today ...", "They're just being boisterous boys" and "Don't you look pretty and sparkly today!" I would certainly be rich by now! These comments are not as outdated as we might think. Many educators regularly use gender as a basis to segregate children, yet we wouldn't dream of using faith or skin colour to do this. We need to be conscious of our use of gendered language and ensure that we are not adding fuel to any stereotypes by the way we talk to our children.

Gender stereotypes

Children use stereotypes in order to understand the world around them by generalising and making assumptions about how the world works. This is developmentally appropriate at a basic level and when children are learning about what makes a boy a boy and a girl a girl. For example, children tend to initially use physical appearance to help them to distinguish between the sexes. They usually make a connection between hair length and gender – boys have short hair and girls have long hair, assuming that all boys have short hair and all girls have long hair. This is sometimes called a gender schema, when children have particular ideas about gender and use these thoughts to structure their thinking (Martin and Halverson, 1981). When they find out something new they either assimilate this learning into their existing thought patterns or accommodate their thinking to allow for the new learning and change their schema slightly.

An example of this is if a young child encounters a girl with very short hair, they would be forgiven for assuming that she is a boy, however, when presented with the fact that this child is actually a girl, they need to change their thinking to allow for this new information. So stereotypes in a way can help to simplify quite complex ideas and can play a key role in simplifying a complex world, however, we need to be careful not to rely on gender stereotypes too rigidly as we must be flexible enough to revise our beliefs when presented with behaviour and preferences that are counter to our ideas. We must not label people or make assumptions based on gender. Generalising about gender diminishes as children grow older as they are able to take into account any counter-stereotypical information they have been given (Banerjee and Lintern, 2000).

It is widely documented that parents treat babies differently depending on their gender (Rubin, Provenzano and Luria, 1974) and that children who engage in typical opposite-sex behaviours or activities tend to be criticised or receive negative attention as a result (Browne, 2004). This is particularly true of boys who engage in activities that would be typically described as feminine, for example, pushing a doll's pram. Girls, by the same token, are not so widely criticised if they decide to start playing football, in fact, sometimes these activities are widely encouraged as society has become more aware of the unequal gender balance within different sports and professions. Thus boys get a raw deal and being a quiet, sensitive boy who prefers to read and colour rather than engage in more physical and sporting activities is still seen by many as atypical. This needs to be addressed if we want to live in a society that is less pressured in terms of gender.

In addition, Browne (2004) observes that when children play in more "unnatural" ways, for example, if girls take on an aggressive role or boys persistently choose more feminine pursuits, adults take notice of this and are more likely to intervene. This could be because this type of play contravenes the adult's feeling of natural play and it could be argued that more stereotypical play "feels" more appropriate for children to engage in. Therefore when children engage in ways that fit with generalisations of boys and girls play, adults accept this play more readily, which, in turn, reinforces the play and becomes a self-fulfilling prophecy. Thus adults need to reflect on their role in relation to children's play to ensure that they are interacting, not interfering (Fisher, 2016). Browne (2004) suggests that superhero play is a powerful medium for exploring femininity and masculinity within the early years.

Young children also use these gender schemas when they think about themselves and their peers, for example: "Pink is for girls, blue is for boys. That ball is pink, so it's for girls." Or "Boys like to play with cars. He must also like cars." Kolberg takes this argument a step further as he suggests that children's gender role development is actually self-socialised as a child might think: "I am a boy, therefore I want to do boy things" (Kohlberg, 1966, p. 89) and this idea then shapes what they do and how they do it. They are intrinsically or extrinsically rewarded for this way of thinking. Children are in control of their own gender identity and create schemas to reinforce their thinking about gender roles and create rules about which toys boys and girls should play with

(Shaffer, 2009). "Long before children have attained gender constancy, they prefer to play with toys traditionally associated with their gender, to model their behavior after same-sex models, and to reward peers for gender-appropriate behavior" (Bussey and Bandura, 1999, p. 678). It is through these ideas that children sometimes form inaccurate thoughts about gender roles and as educators we need to suggest alternative points of view.

Case study – addressing gender stereotypes from a parent's perspective: Catherine's story

When Catherine started nursery at age three, some of the boys in her setting told her that she wasn't allowed to like superheroes because she was a girl. Up until this point, superheroes had never been a particularly big part of our lives but this was a red rag to a bull for me as her mum, and I immediately went online and bought her a Wonder Woman costume! We talked about why the boys had said this and explored the idea that some people have a misconception that there are boys things and girls things – like toys and colours and interests – but that it's OK for her to choose her own likes and dislikes and that if she likes superheroes that's absolutely fine. I spoke to the staff at her nursery, too; they were horrified that Catherine had been told this and promised to do what they could to promote better understanding and inclusion in the class. They began a theme looking at superheroes that culminated in a superhero Christmas party where Catherine proudly wore her Wonder Woman costume and the staff wore capes and superhero temporary tattoos. The boys were encouraged to see that it was OK for girls to like these things, too.

All went well until the day she wore a Spider-Man t-shirt to nursery. This brought a whole new aspect to the discussion, as the boys now said that she could only like girl superheroes because she was a girl and that boy superheroes like Spider-Man were only for boys. So we talked some more at home and I put out a rallying cry to friends and family to show Catherine that males could like female superheroes and vice versa. I was rewarded with numerous photos and videos of all of her amazing grown-up role models wearing an array of t-shirts and costumes, including a favourite uncle wearing a Wonder Woman t-shirt. I wanted to show her that these wonderful people who she looked up to weren't afraid of a stupid stereotype and that they could like whichever heroes they wanted. I'll never forget the look on her face when I showed her all the photos people had sent me; it was priceless. And her love of superheroes, male and female, continues four years on, along with her love of sparkly things, cuddly toys, climbing trees, insects, muddy puddles, drawing, yoga, martial arts – she knows that toys are just toys, colours are just colours and that sometimes people can be very small minded.

Throughout this whole episode, the staff at her nursery worked in partnership with me and were very supportive. They addressed these stereotypes in the setting while we also discussed these ideas at home.

Here are some ideas that will help you to support children in relation to gender:

- Allow children to play with gender and accept their choices, if a boy wants to dress as Wonder Woman, that's OK, just as we should accept a girl dressing as Spider-Man.
- Allow opportunities for children to celebrate as well as resist gendered ways of playing.
- Reflect on how you react to children playing in gendered ways or children who resist playing in these ways.
- Ensure that all practitioners in your setting have an understanding of gender issues.
- Help children to use inclusive rather than gendered language and model this.
- Practice flexible gender roles through pretend play, i.e. boy can be a caring mother figure and female practitioner can be Superman.
- Talk with the children and encourage discussion about ideas relating to gender. Can boys and girls play the same games? Visit the same places? Are there any times when this boys and girls need to be separated?
- Observe the children as they play and make a note of the different play choices that both boys and girls make. Track where they play and how they engage with the resources and then compare these data for boys and girls. What do you notice?
- Join in with children's play and role model by facilitating storylines and scaffold their learning.
- Avoid making generalisations about how boys and girls play as this will reduce the likelihood of creating gender stereotypes.

What does this mean in practice?

We must remember that within ECE, the workforce is almost exclusively female with recent figures implying that only 2% of childcare practitioners are male (Simon, Owen and Hollingworth, 2016). We must ensure that we are making every effort to provide appropriately for all children and reflect on our own attitudes and practice. Are we always comfortable with the types of play that boys (and girls) engage in? If we're honest, do we approve and accept the interests of all of our children equally? How do we feel about the behaviours we label as belonging to boys? Do we treat some boys differently, especially if we are uncomfortable with their behaviour? An honest analysis of our feelings and actions is probably the most effective starting point in relation to developing our practice around gender to benefit both boys and girls. Chapter 2 considers this in relation to aggression and rough and tumble play.

If you do not have any male members of staff, one useful strategy is to introduce male role models in terms of visitors and volunteers, for example, granddads or older brothers. Can you encourage a friend's child to volunteer to come in and read to the children or play with them every couple of weeks? Or organise a "Dads' and Kids' Day"? Many secondary schools encourage their students to volunteer for schemes such as the Duke of Edinburgh's Award and will release them to spend time in your setting.

When we are planning for boys and girls and resourcing the environment, we cannot rely on the fact that everything is accessible to boys and girls and suggest that therefore we are providing equality of opportunity for them because we know that young children tend to choose gender-specific activities and resources and therefore we may need to support them to engage in other activities and widen their experiences.

In the light of our female heavy childcare workforce, here are some additional ideas of how to support boys and reduce the gender gap:

- Use superhero play as an opportunity to explore femininity and masculinity and gender issues.
- Actively try to increase the presence of men in our settings.
- Train all staff in issues relating to gender development.
- Make the setting as "boy friendly" as possible; you could enlist the help of older boys.
- Use strategies that have been proven to engage boys such as incorporating movement and hands-on activities into all areas of learning and development.
- Focus on equality of opportunity for boys that is not providing the same for boys and girls.
- Encourage boys and girls to interact with one another and challenge any stereotypes you encounter.
- Positively reinforce and praise play when boys and girls are enjoying playing together.
- Use active learning tasks and plan multisensory activities; target setting, monitoring and mentoring; using older children as male role models.
- Have high expectations of boys and their abilities.
- Effectively use visual media, technology and props to aid learning.
- Provide opportunities to practise fine motor skills in ways that engage them.
- Recognise the difference between aggressive play and violence.
- Tap into their fascinations and interests.
- Speak clearly to boys, lower your tone, slow your speech and use fewer words.
- Offer adequate space to play in and time to engage the play.
- Encourage outdoor play or gross motor play before any activities that require them to be stationary.
- Give children warnings before transitions.
- Keep carpet time/group times as short as possible.
- Praise boys and encourage competition and team playing/collaboration.

Despite the positive changes within society and the research that celebrates our similarities, gender is regularly portrayed on a more commercial level in more stereotypical ways, for example, shops regularly divide their wares into boys' and girls' sections, male superheroes tend to be strong and very masculine and female superheroes take on many of these more masculine attributes, albeit in a very shapely and unrealistic body. Therefore, although superheroes provide us with a great opportunity to discuss gender issues, we need to be aware of the many stereotypes that they may endorse as well as challenge. Women may be portrayed as sexy or "damsels in distress" and the majority of superhero characters are strong men who display very masculine tendencies. These stereotypes are easier to avoid if you use heroes who are aimed specifically at younger children, for example, Go Jetters or PJ Masks or focus on real-life heroes (see Chapter 6).

Early childhood educators need to counter negative influences or those that reinforce gender stereotypes, for example, in order to redress the balance, Wonder Woman can be included in any superhero-themed play and practitioners can ensure that Superman saves both genders from peril. In addition, because superhero play is often exclusively seen as a boys' interest and activity that boys engage in, we need to ensure that our settings counter this mindset, enabling girls to engage in this play and offering strong female and male role models, as we saw in Catherine's story above.

Case study – Pebbles childcare

Among all of the various dressing-up clothes on offer, Amelia instantly selects this outfit and says: "I am Supergirl because I have all of the powers and help all of the people!"

We also need to be cautious when we are choosing activities and resourcing our learning environment. Throughout my career with children and in parenting my own three girls, I have insisted that there are no boys' or girls' toys, just toys and no colours reserved for one sex, all colours are for everyone. It is important that these messages get through to our children within our settings. Ensure that our resources are free from stereotypical images and that we are aware of the biases that can so easily creep in. We can focus on strength in terms of character rather than muscles and think about our own super-skills. Chapter 10 considers this in more detail. Superhero play is like a gift, offering us many opportunities to work towards gender equity and explore issues related to gender in our settings.

In summary

In answering if superhero play is a question of gender – the short answer is often yes! But it shouldn't be. Both boys and girls enjoy all types of play that fall under this bracket and superhero play can provide us as educators with an opportunity to explore notions relating to equity and challenge gender stereotypes. We know that children are a product of both nature and nurture and we have a part to play in ensuring that the messages we are giving our children are the messages we want them to receive.

Questions for reflection

1. How will you support both boys and girls to join in and learn through superhero play?
2. What messages does this type of play give your children in relation to gender, overtly or covertly?
3. How can you ensure a balance between competent, strong girl superheroes as well as the damsel in distress and how can you be sensitive to children's needs as their understanding of gender develops?
4. Reflect on your own relationships with boys in your setting. Are there any aspects you want to develop to support boys further?

References

Banerjee, R. (2005) Gender identity and the development of gender roles. In Ding, S. and Littleton, S. (Eds.) *Children's Personal and Social Development (Child Development)*. Maidenhead: Open University Press

Banerjee, R. and Lintern, V. (2000) Boys will be boys: the effect of social evaluation concerns on gender-typing, *Social Development*, *9*(3), pp. 397–408

Bayley, R. and Featherstone, S. (2010) *The Cleverness of Boys*. London: A & C Black Publishers Limited

Browne, N. (2004) *Gender Equity in the Early Years*. Maidenhead: Open University Press

DfE (2018) EYFSP results in England, 2018. Retrieved from https://www.gov.uk/ government/ statistics/early-years-foundation-stage-profile-results-2017-to-2018

Bussey, K and Bandura, A. (1999) Social cognitive theory of gender development and differentiation, *Psychological Review*, *106*(4), pp. 676–713

Fisher, J. (2016) *Interacting or Interfering? Improving Interactions in the Early Years*. Maidenhead: Open University Press

Joel, D., Persico, A., Salhov, M., Berman, Z., Oligschlger, S., Meilijson, I. et al. (2018) Analysis of human brain structure reveals that the brain "types" typical of males are also typical of females, and vice versa, *Frontiers in Human Neuroscience*, *12*, p. 399

Kohlberg, L. (1966) A cognitive-developmental analysis of children's sex-role concepts and attitudes. In Maecoby, E. E. (Ed.) *The Development of Sex Differences*. Stanford, CA: Stanford University Press

Martin, C. and Halverson, C. (1981) A schematic processing model of sex typing and stereotyping in children, *Child Development*, *52*(4)

McConaghy, M. (1979) Gender permanence and the genital basis of gender: stages in the development of constancy of gender identity, *Child Development*, (4), p. 1223

Richoz, A., Quinn P., Hillairet de Boisferon A., Berger C., Loevenbruck, H., Lewkowicz, D.et al. (2017) Audio-visual perception of gender by infants emerges earlier for adult-directed speech, *PLOS ONE 12*(1)

Rosen, M. (2007) *This Is Our House*. London: Walker Books

Rubin, J., Provenzano, F. and Luria, Z. (1974) The eye of the beholder: parents' views on sex of newborns, *American Journal of Orthopsychiatry*, *44*, pp. 512–519

Shaffer, D. (2009) *Social and Personality Development*, 6th ed. Belmont, CA: Wadsworth Cengage Learning

Simon, A., Owen, C. and Hollingworth, K. (2016) Is the "quality" of preschool childcare, measured by the qualifications and pay of the childcare workforce, improving in Britain? *American Journal of Educational Research*, *4*(1), pp. 11–17

Stonewall (2017) *Getting Started: Celebrating Difference and Challenging Gender Stereotypes in the Early Years Foundation Stage*. Retrieved from https://www.stonewall.org.uk/sites/default/files/getting_started_early_years.pdf

Thompson, M. and Barker, T. (2008) *It's a Boy: Your Son's Development from Birth to Age 18*. New York: Ballantine Books

Wilson, G. (2006) *Breaking through Barriers to Boys' Achievement: Developing a Caring Masculinity*. London: Network Continuum Education

5 "Superheroes? British values?"

British values and early years provision

Dr Kay Mathieson

I have asked my esteemed colleague and friend Kay Mathieson to write this chapter as she regularly links superheroes with British values when delivering training. When I first heard about this I thought: "Superheroes? British values? I'd love to find out more about this!" So when the opportunity came for me to write this book, I immediately asked Kay to write about this interesting way of engaging with the Prevent duty and teaching children about British values.

British values and early years provision

> Early years providers serve arguably the most vulnerable and impressionable members of society ... Early years providers already focus on children's personal social and emotional development. The early years foundation stage framework supports early years providers to do this in an age appropriate way, through ensuring children learn right from wrong, mix and share with other children and value other's views, know about similarities and differences between themselves and others, and challenge negative attitudes and stereotypes.
>
> (Revised Prevent Duty Guidance, Home Office, 2015, p. 10)

There is regularly concern raised about young children's social understanding, specifically, early influences on their behaviour and moral awareness. Early childhood educators have supportive guidance in the form of the Early Years Foundation Stage Framework (Department for Education (DfE), 2017) and Development Matters document (Early Education, 2012). Beyond early years, schools are required to continue age-appropriate, proactive engagement with children to extend their understanding of rights responsibilities and social connections as the *Revised Prevent Duty Guidance* (Home Office, 2015, p. 10) states:

> All publicly-funded schools in England are required by law to teach a broad and balanced curriculum which promotes the spiritual, moral, cultural, mental and physical development of pupils and prepares them for the opportunities, responsibilities and experiences of life. They must also promote community cohesion. Independent schools set their own curriculum but must comply with the Independent School Standards, which include an explicit requirement to promote fundamental British values as part of broader requirements relating to the quality of education and to promoting the spiritual, moral, social and cultural development of pupils.

During inspections, the Office for Standards in Education (Ofsted) will look for evidence of the following aspects of practice related to promoting British values and personal, social and emotional development:

Effectiveness of leadership and management (p. 31):

- Actively promote equality and diversity, tackle poor behaviour towards others, including bullying and discrimination, and reduce any differences in outcomes between groups of children

- Actively promote British values
- Make sure that arrangements to protect children meet all statutory and other government requirements, promote their welfare and prevent radicalisation and extremism

Personal development, behaviour and welfare (p. 40):

- Personal development, so that they are well prepared to respect others and contribute to wider society and life in Britain.

(Ofsted, 2018)

What does this mean for professionals working in the EYFS?

It is tempting to think that our youngest children are too young to engage in such adult sounding "big picture" concerns. However, professionally we know that early experiences can have lifelong consequences. It is therefore important that adults working with young children challenge their own thinking and understanding of these issues. Working together practitioners are able to establish a setting culture that reflects a conscious, well-considered approach to making these "human values" the daily lived experience of children and adults in the setting community.

Children in the EYFS are at the very beginning of understanding these complex concepts. Attending childcare provision where they are appropriately and consciously present will positively support each child's emerging awareness of community cohesion. As listed below, there are many opportunities to demonstrate each of these values appropriately in our setting.

Democracy:

- Facilitating meaningful choices that affect our experience.
- Listening to the views of others.
- Considering the consequences of our choices on others.
- Recognising the merits of others' views.
- Amending how we think.
- Weighing up the facts before making a choice.
- Giving reasons for our actions and decisions.
- Admitting we have made a mistake.
- Being able to change our minds without losing face or being ridiculed.

- Going with the majority view.
- Making a case against the majority view.
- Compromising to resolve an issue.

The rule of law:

- Being involved in creating appropriate rules that help everyone to be together.
- Creating a commonly understood way to resolve conflicts.
- Experiencing responsibilities and consequences related to agreed rules.
- Being able to question and alter rules where this will improve the experience of all involved.

Individual liberty:

- Recognising the impact of what we say on others.
- Freedom of speech and thought, being listened to, being supported to hear others.
- Recognising the impact of what we think on our own experience.
- Seeing another's perspective.
- Recognising and ensuring fairness and compassion in problem solving.

Mutual respect and tolerance of different faiths and beliefs:

- Recognising and being able to learn about similarities and differences between individuals and groups.
- Realising that there is seldom "one right way" but alternative journeys and different outcomes.
- Being valued, respected as an individual as well as valuing and respecting others.
- Experiencing positive models of collaboration and problem solving rather than power and control attributed to being bigger, louder, scarier etc.

These examples are by no means exhaustive but have one key requirement in common. In order to sustain the positive influence, they must apply to all members of the setting community, adults and children alike. This creates a dynamic process where those with less, more or different experience are able to accept, challenge and question to deepen the collective ethos. Fundamental to this evolving process is the need for realistic expectations that are based on secure knowledge of child development and the complexities of personal, social and emotional understanding.

Child development

Relating with others in a variety of ways is essential to human life. First, as a baby being nurtured and cared for, then learning the complexities of ongoing relationships with family and friends. Finally, as we become more independent, extending this beyond home to our own friends and acquaintances (for further reading, see Carpendale and Lewis, 2006; Dunn, 2004; Hughes, 2011).

Developmental changes in social and emotional awareness, understanding and communication are dramatic during our earliest years. One significant change in a child's world view, brought about by the gradual evolving of so-called "theory of mind understanding" is a key example. The realisation that another human being can be thinking something completely different from you is the beginning of a lifelong journey of seeking to understand others' perspectives. Chapter 6 explores theory of mind in further detail.

In common with other developmental changes, exploring how others think about the world is demonstrated in children's play. "Standing in someone else's shoes" is most obvious in role play where a child "becomes" the fairy, monster, hero, parent, dog etc. As children explore this process they have a vehicle for some increasingly complex thinking:

- What might it be like to be this character in this situation?
- How do I feel when I am this character?
- How do others react when I am this character?
- Is it different from the way they react when I am "me"?

Equally, being someone else in a pretend/fantasy context offers opportunities to explore emotions:

- Playing out the angry/sad/scared adult, or child.
- How does it feel to be, the baddie, the goodie, scared, brave, sad?

Recognising that all humans have the capacity to feel the full range of emotions is fundamental to developing and maintaining empathy. Understanding that those demonstrating anger, control, confidence or fear are showing only one aspect of themselves and that in different circumstances other facets will be displayed supports our view of individuals as like ourselves. This is more likely to evoke our feelings of empathy than if we categorise someone as "angry" or "frightened" without the capacity for other emotions.

So, from around two years onwards awareness of others becomes a fascinating and bewildering experience. Beginning with awareness of others' intentions through to recognition that "displayed" emotions may not be "felt" emotions challenges our ability to predict and process the social implications and required response (Wilson and Wilson,

2015). Getting it "wrong" in a play context is infinitely preferable than risking it in a real-life situation. Given that each individual has such different experiences, worldviews and levels of understanding how then do we manage to "get along" with most people most of the time?

Within a family the older, more experienced humans demonstrate and establish ways of relating, distributing resources and responsibilities that are influenced by patterns from their own growing up. This sharing of ideas and ways of being are seldom conscious or discussed, they are "just the way we are". When a child and family become involved beyond the home with community groups and childcare provision, there is a coming together of often very different expectations. Children take time to make sense of the similarities and differences between these experiences. Role play and pretend play are dynamic opportunities to work out some of the variations and continuities between their experiences.

On a wider stage, children become increasingly aware that there are "rules" in each context. Initially, these "rules" are assumed to be equally applied to all and at all times. This is followed by the discovery that some rules are negotiable. This insight initially adds confusion, as children seek to confirm which rules are absolute or negotiable and if these are dependent on the adult present, the context or are just random. Predictability is increased by testing out each rule, with different adults at different times, looking for patterns and continuity if not consistency. None of this is conscious but adults find it extremely annoying at times!

Integral to this process is the development of the idea of there being "right" and "wrong" actions. Again there is confusion about context, some actions may be perceived as "right" at home but not at Granny's, nursery, childminders etc., and vice versa. Some actions are "right" if one individual does it but not if another does. As children begin to recognise these anomalies they also begin to develop their own moral awareness and thinking (Dunn et al., 1991).

There are distinct aspects of morality that children (and adults) are working to understand:

- Morality of justice – this involves being able to apply "fair" treatment to a range of situations.
- Moral dilemmas and principles – although principles may be easier to talk about, e.g. respect for life, dilemmas arise that challenge such broad ideals, such as making decisions about who should be given scarce, expensive medication a young child or an elderly adult patient.
- Moral reasoning – is the process we develop in our thinking and articulation about how we might apply a moral principle to a specific case. (Carpendale and Lewis, 2006)

With support from insightful adults, children begin to explore and develop the ability to recognise moral challenges. By definition, a "moral challenge or dilemma" does not have an easy or straightforward "right" answer. The process of shared thinking that the adult is able to create allows for the introduction of a variety of "possible" solutions to be considered. Integral to this discussion is the need to justify, clarify and refine our thinking about acceptable or unacceptable solutions. For the adult involved, the role is clearly about encouraging "possibility thinking" rather than making sure that the children come to a preconceived "right" answer. For the children, the feeling of having an equal voice to the adult, listening to and being listened to, is a powerful support to this complex thinking process.

This skill set is also something that has been found to be central to a child's ability to sustain peer friendships through differences of opinion and daily conflicts. In fact, in their research, Malti, Gummerman and Buchmann (2009) showed that six-year-old children's "moral motivation" included the capacity to provide appropriate moral explanations for conflicts. Children who were able to give such explanations were also more likely to demonstrate prosocial behaviour among their peers. Therefore, understanding in the moral domain may thus be considered as crucial to children's learning about everyday conflict resolution and therefore their maintenance of peer relationships (Malti et al., 2009).

There have been three well-known considerations of the generational recurrence of war, weapon and superhero play in young children. Holland (2003), reacting to a significant period of such play being "banned" in early years provision, argues for adults to value and engage in this play rather than pushing it "underground". Rich (2003), takes the view that the shared storytelling experience allows children to work out their understanding of situations together. Sharing ideas and thinking about how the story should unfold is undoubtedly a positive experience supporting language development, thinking skills and self-esteem.

Popper (2013) takes the thinking a stage further arguing that superhero and weapon play is a vehicle for children to explore "right and wrong" and moral dilemmas. He looks in depth at the story structure and how superheroes demonstrate the application of moral principles and the resolution of natural order in a predictable format.

Chapter 2 draws on various pieces of research that have looked into aggressive behaviour in young children and considers the potential benefits of weapon play.

Making sense of the world

There is an age-/understanding-related gradation through superhero stories and characters, from Numberjacks to Captain Marvel characters, each creating a structure for children to explore particular aspects of good, bad, right and wrong. Essentially, there are "goodies and baddies" who are, at least temporarily, in opposition to each other. The baddies generally take resources, people or territory.

Through such stories children are able to experience and explore, in a safe context.

Dilemmas:

- The rule of law – whose rules/laws?
- Are all rules equal?
- Are they applied all the time?
- Are they applied to all people?

Individual liberty:

- Why might it be OK to "lock up" the "baddies"?
- Why might the "baddies" "lock up" or take people away?
- Is it OK for anyone to say anything about anyone else?

Identifying dilemmas:

- What is the moral issue at stake in this story?
- What are the "baddies" thinking about this issue?
- What are the "goodies" thinking about this issue?
- How can both groups think they are "right"?

Reconciliation:

- What are the possible outcomes?
- What would need to happen to enable a resolution acceptable to all?
- What happens if the groups do not trust one another to comply with the agreed resolution?

The skills and collaborative thinking that can be demonstrated through such play include:

- Changed awareness – such as recognising that "baddies" can do good things and vice versa.
- Compromise – there doesn't have to be one "winner", together we can work things out.

- Cooperating in a shared game – making "rules", negotiating changes to rules as the game progresses, accepting ideas from a range of players not just the loudest/most dominant.
- Staying in role – maintaining a character requires self-regulation, awareness of self and holding in mind how the character might respond.
- Resolution – mutual respect, tolerance, the bigger picture reflecting on the moral principles and how hard/easy it was to apply them.
- A character who has lost a battle but will come back for more.
- Demonstrating moral thinking.
- Strategic problem solving.
- Complex perspective taking.
- Justifying "nearly good" and "nearly bad" actions.
- Thinking through the consequences for self and others.
- Consistency of moral stance.
- Making difficult decisions where no one "wins".
- Appropriate use of power.

Adults who are knowledgeable and aware of the backstory and characteristics of the particular superheroes that the children are engaging with are more likely to be able to scaffold a child's thinking appropriately. Professional understanding of child development will then facilitate tuning in to a child's current understanding and recognising possible ways to stretch their thinking. Some examples follow.

Story structure related to superheroes:

- Goodie, baddie, problem, rescue, solution, moral principle
- Main character with a purpose
- Defined moral stance
- Main protagonist/enemy
- A range of special powers but may have "conditions"
- The ultimate "nemesis"
- A scenario depicting "good" and "evil" with varying levels of dilemma depending on the complexity of the character
- Framework for thinking, not a writing activity

- Co-construction, a social "joint" think
- Must have a resolution to be satisfying
- Alternative possible solutions
- Being true to the established character
- How have we outwitted villains before?
- Which strategies have been successful?
- What does it feel like to be a goodie/baddy
- What would a compromise look like?
- What if the baddy wins?
- What happens if special powers are combined against a common enemy?

Getting stuck at bish, bash, bosh

Sometimes superhero play can become merely a re-enactment of the inevitable "chase" or "fight" scene. This usually occurs where the children are developmentally ready for accepting new information or structure into their play but are finding it difficult to take this next step by themselves. As a result the repetitive actions become the play rather than being able to work with the unfolding adventure.

To help things progress, adults can support with prompts at the beginning of the play to help the children consider:

- Who the characters are.
- What they are trying to do.

Ideally, the adult role becomes that of play companion where they engage as a character in the play helping the children to develop their ideas through prompts and questions. For example, checking understanding when the fight scene ends up with "you're dead!" This can be challenged with the idea that most superheroes do not kill people. Familiarisation with comic stories and making up picture storyboards related to current favourite superheroes to extend understanding can be used as a significant influence on the children's play. A key feature of the adult role is to extend thinking together for example engaging in conversation related to open out children's thinking:

- What if Superman didn't feel well?
- What if the goodie did something bad?

Case study – home setting

These children were keen to play at being superheroes but were unsure of what to do. The adult asked them about what they thought superheroes do and how they act. The children decided that superheroes help and rescue people. Later on Olivia was observed rescuing Dexter on the slide. They took it in turns to be the superhero rescuing and the child in distress.

- What if the baddies did something good?
- What makes a superhero?
- What does a superhero's name communicate?
- What does she/he look like?
- What special powers does the superhero have and what are the rules for using them?
- Who are the superhero's friends?
- Who are baddies in this story? Why are they baddies?

As the stories develop in children's play some key aspects of the nature of conflict become clearer, for example in terms of resolution "baddies" can be:

- Outwitted
- Over powered
- Reformed

The final solution can include experience of:

- Negotiation
- Compromise
- Refining our communication of the "problem"
- Being able to tell our story coherently to engage others

Superheroes do not have to work alone. Exploring with the children the benefits of teamwork and collaboration, especially with confident characters who can dominate play scenarios, can create a significant change of perspective. In a superhero team:

- No one character has all the skills/talents/attributes needed to resolve the problem.
- Selecting a team for a specific purpose/problem, but all of equal value as individuals, for example in Paw Patrol, is a skill in itself.
- Effective teamwork will most likely require superheroes who have a similar moral purpose working.

One step at a time ...

Our setting ethos can be difficult to ascertain as we are both experiencing and contributing to it on a daily basis. Taking every opportunity to gain insights from visitors, parents and children about their own experience of coming to and being in our environment is essential. By consciously reflecting on this range of views, we can challenge and embed the aspects of our practice in relation to the British values of democracy, rule of law, individual liberty, mutual respect and tolerance in an appropriate and meaningful way (Action for Children, 2016).

Young children learn through play and in ECE adults create opportunities for increasingly complex play and child led learning. The complex issues involved in establishing and maintaining relationships include the dilemmas, moral principles, collaboration that are characteristic of British values as set out in the Prevent Duty Guidance (Home Office, 2015).

Child-led superhero play offers a context that can be used to constructively explore emotions, motivations and dilemmas in an emotionally safe environment. Where practitioners take the time to explore with the children, the characteristics and moral principles of the superheroes they are interested in, this learning increases in complexity to become a profound experience for children.

Case study – reception class dilemmas

Aunt May has asked Peter (a.k.a. Spiderman) why he is so tired ...
Well...? Why are you so tired Peter?
Should Peter lie to protect his secret identity?

Several children were engaged in goodies and baddies play that the practitioners found to be repetitive and lacking in purpose. They decided to focus on the values that superheroes promote and talked to the children about creating their own superhero identities. The children needed to decide what their powers were and the values that they stood for.

To think about this further and to link in with Philosophy for Children, they introduced some storyboards that contained moral dilemmas, for example, Wonder Woman had the option to save the world but in doing so Superman would be banished forever to another planet or Spider-Man had been out all night fighting baddies but what should he tell his Aunt when she asked why he was so tired? These comic strip-style stories were designed to get the children talking and worked a treat!

Linking superheroes with British values can feel like making play a serious matter – in terms of learning, it is serious but this does not mean adults should not engage playfully with the children. Humour is an essential part of playing together and one of the great benefits of being able to play with serious aspects of human relationships in a pretend context is to try things out and make mistakes without real-life consequences.

A major factor linking superhero play to the real life of a setting includes supporting a child's understanding of, and skills related to conflict resolution. Every day sees a conflict when resources, adult time, space etc., have to be shared. By establishing a consistent approach to resolving conflict we can significantly influence our setting ethos. An example would be teaching children a simple five-step process of:

1. *Stop* – say and demonstrate hand signal.
2. *Listen* – recognise that those involved will not give the same account but need to have their opportunity to speak.
3. *Think* – establish a minimum of two possible solutions for children to negotiate.
4. *Do* – carry out the agreed solution.
5. *Tell* – check in with an adult to see that it has worked.

As the children become used to the process they are able to develop their skill through, first, suggesting increasingly appropriate and creative solutions and then taking on responsibility for the "stop" and gradually each of the remaining steps. Chapter 8 explores another strategy we can teach children, called the problem-solving approach to conflict resolution, which also develops children's skills and over time enables them to resolve conflicts for themselves.

As always, the most effective early years practice starts from the children. Developing the play they are interested and intrigued by is demonstrating respect for their ideas and personal views as well as enhancing their self-esteem and feelings of wellbeing as they work through ideas and concepts that help them understand their world and relationships. So, the children won't need convincing but colleagues and parents might – superhero play has often had "bad press" so it is worth thinking carefully about how you might redress this perspective. Gathering examples of the increasing social skill, understanding and awareness of the complex thinking that children are demonstrating may be your starting point. Following this with a professional explanation of the links between superhero play and British values can increase the value attributed to a child's play. But most of all working with parents exploring the detail of how to respond and support a child's learning through superhero play will be the most practical and effective approach.

Questions for reflection

1 To what extent have you embedded the British values of democracy, rule of law, individual liberty, mutual respect and tolerance into your practice?
2 In what ways can you use superhero play as an opportunity to teach children about these values?
3 How can you extend children's play beyond, "bish, bash, bosh"?

References

Action for Children (2016) *Fundamental British Values in the Early Years.* Foundation Years. London: Action for Children. Available from www.foundationyears.org.uk/ wp-content/ uploads/2017/08/Fundamental-British-Values-in-the-Early-Years-2017.pdf

Carpendale, J. I. M. and Lewis, C. (2006) *How Children Develop Social Understanding.* Oxford: Blackwell Publishing

Department for Education (DfE) (2017) *Early Years Foundation Stage.* London: DfE

Dunn, J. (2004) *Children's Friendships: The Beginnings of Intimacy.* Oxford: Blackwell

Dunn, J., Brown, J., Slomkowski, C., Tesla, C. and Youngblade, L. (1991) Young children's understanding of other people's feelings and beliefs: individual differences and their antecedence, *Child Development, 62*(6), pp. 1352–1366

Early Education (2012) *Development Matters in the Early Years Foundation Stage*. London: DfE
Holland, P. (2003) *We Don't Play with Guns Here: War, Weapon and Superhero Play in the Early Years*. Maidenhead: Open University Press
Home Office (2015) Revised Prevent Duty Guidance for England and Wales. Retrieved from https://www.gov.uk/government/publications/prevent-duty-guidance
Hughes, C. (2011) *Social Understanding and Social Lives*. Hove: Psychology Press
Malti, T., Gummerman, M. and Buchmann, M. (2009) Children's moral motivation, sympathy and prosocial behaviour, *Child Development, 80*(2), pp. 442–460
Ofsted (2018) Early Years Inspection Handbook. Retrieved from https://www.gov.uk/government/publications/inspecting-registered-early-years-providers-guidance-for-inspectors
Popper, S. (2013) *Rethinking Superhero and Weapon Play*. Maidenhead: Open University Press
Rich, D. (2003) Bang, bang! Gun play, and why children need it, *Early Education Journal,* Summer 2003. Retrieved from http://dianerich.co.uk/pdf/bang%20bang%20gun% 20play%20and%20why%20children%20need%20it.pdf
Wilson, R. L. and Wilson, R. (2015) *Understanding Emotional Development*. Hove: Psychology Press

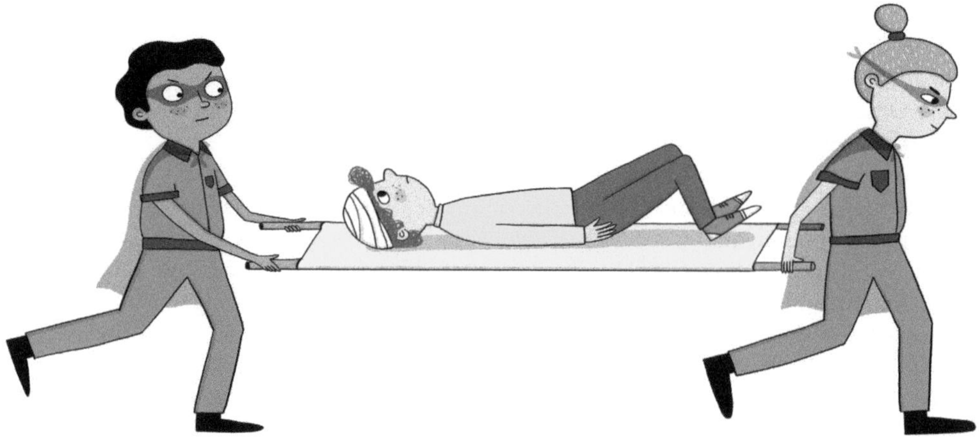

6 "My dad is my hero!"

Exploring the real heroes in our lives

Introduction

Children are surrounded by stories of heroism in real life. Take for example the horrific events at the Grenfell Tower fire in London. The firefighters showed bravery, emotional resilience and physical strength amid such terrifying circumstances. We can share examples of how ordinary people can, and do, do extraordinary things. We do not want to limit superheroes to those with superpowers or an extra human strength; instead, we want our children to develop a growth mindset where the sky's the limit or, rather, where there are no limits! This will require us role modelling, sharing stories of adults and children overcoming adversity and problem solving in everyday scenarios.

I spent time in a setting, while researching superheroes for this book, observing children and talking to them about their heroes and heroism. While scooting in the outdoor area Kyle (aged nearly four) talked to me enthusiastically about his Dad who was his hero. He said: "My Daddy can stand on a scooter handle. He can save people. He jumped from Bath to France and he jumped from a house to France and to America and then to England. He bumped into someone on the beach getting their picnic."

Kyle demonstrates his knowledge of heroes as he talks about saving people and also shares how amazing his father is by talking about the wonderful things he can do, demonstrating his strength and super ability to balance! Children regularly fabricate things (Evans and Lee, 2013), so it doesn't matter about the truth behind these statements, what is important is how Kyle holds his Dad in high regard and I'm sure his Dad was thrilled to hear this too! This same child told me that his sister is the one who always drives the family car. It turns out that he does indeed have a sister, but she is only 18 months older than him and just five years old, so it is highly unlikely that she drives the family car! In order for a child to actively deceive someone they need some elements of theory of mind. Kyle might have been wanting to impress me about his Dad or perhaps he wanted to say something that would sum up his intense feelings about how great his Dad is. In this context, his Dad is his hero and the "lie" that he told can be categorised along with fantasy thoughts and pretence.

Developing theory of mind

Talwar and Lee (2008, p. 877) state that: "Children's 'primary lies' begin around 2–3 years of age when children are first able to deliberately make factually untrue statements." Stating untruths is a common thing for young children to do and it needs to be distinguished from actively lying when someone is saying something untrue to deliberately deceive someone else. In order to deliberately lie children need an understanding that other people have thoughts and feelings that are different to theirs. This is called theory of mind and is all about social interaction. It begins developing at a young age when babies of around six months old can distinguish between animate and inanimate objects. As they grow and develop, young children will be able to engage in joint attention with other people (around 12 months) and learn how to sense the direction of another's gaze (around 18 months). The ability to engage in pretend play and imagine that an object is something else (around two years) also contributes to their understanding of theory of mind.

However, it really starts to develop more fully at around four years old when children start to recognise that other people have their own thoughts, feelings and beliefs. They can also begin to understand that sometimes someone has a false belief. Imagine you open your favourite box of chocolates to find that it has conkers inside. Your colleague comes in and looks at the box – what do they think will be inside? Chocolates? This is an example of a false belief, where someone believes something to be true that is not true because they do not have the same knowledge as you.

Research into theory of mind often looks at this understanding of false beliefs and uses a simple test to see at what age children understand this concept. In one such test, a tube of Smarties is shown to a child, then the tube is opened and they find that the Smarties have been replaced with something else. They are asked what their friend, who has not yet seen what is inside the tube, would guess is in the tube. When these false belief activities are completed with three-year-old children, they are not able to guess correctly, whereas most five-year-olds realise that another person does not have their knowledge. This involves predicting what one person thinks, feels and believes about what another person is thinking, feeling and believing.

Theory of mind also involves complex language such as idioms, metaphors and sarcasm, which can usually be understood at around six or seven years old. This is why when an adult says something such as *it's raining cats and dogs*, we find our young children run to the window to look! Another aspect of theory of mind that doesn't develop until over nine years of age is our understanding of "faux pas" or the embarrassing and tactless comments that people can make in social situations.

I was reminded of children's lack of understanding of theory of mind and also our ability as adults to put our foot in it, when a reception class teacher shared with me how Matthew, a child in her class, had told her all about the new baby that his mummy was going to have. He excitedly talked about becoming a big brother, what they were going to call the baby and when Mummy would bring him home. The teacher listened with interest and at parent's evening later that week congratulated Matthew's parents on their forthcoming arrival, to find, to her horror, that this had been a total fabrication and Matthew had completely made this up!

Here are some ideas of activities to try that will support children with their developing theory of mind:

- Help children to recognise different facial expressions and follow eye gaze by playing "hotter and colder" with facial expression and eye gaze to help child find a hidden toy.
- Overemphasise your body language and ask the children to guess how you feel.
- Play a guess the gesture game asking the children to work out what you are trying to say by your gestures alone.
- Play the "what if?" game e.g. What if I were singing loudly and mummy was trying to get my baby sister to sleep. What should I do?
- Engage in pretend play and fantasy play, superheroes are a great context for this.
- Read stories and talk about what a character might do next, how they feel and what could happen …
- Tell jokes, use figurative language and idioms, explaining what you mean.
- Plan activities that encourage children to think about feelings and emotions and what they mean.
- Explain other people's behaviour in past, present and future scenarios.
- Use social stories or choose specific stories that help you to unpick elements of social interaction to help children to understand why people act the way they do.

- Use the language associated with thinking, feeling and believing: feel, forgot, think, know, guess, thought, believe, understand, excited, angry, sad, happy etc.
- Use superhero storylines to discuss moral stories with children.

Real-life heroes

Kyle looked on his Dad as his hero and many of our children will look up to other people as their heroes. Sometimes these heroes are fictional, like Superman, sometimes they are famous, like a pop star or footballer, and sometimes they are heroes from our everyday lives, like Kyle's Dad or Uncle Fred! One idea is to talk to children about heroism, who real-life heroes are and what makes them special. Harris defines "everyday heroes" as "heroes (in the local community or among the students) who are not wearing costumes and masks" (2016, p. 212). You might like to explain that heroes come in all shapes and sizes and many are people whom we might meet every day and who look after us, for example, mummies, daddies, doctors and nurses. Some heroes can be famous such as sportspeople, pop stars or Olympic champions and others can be individuals who overcome adversity or do something very special to help others. You could encourage children to draw a picture of their hero or make a card for their hero and invite them to talk about why they are great.

When discussing heroes with young children, here are a few questions that you might want to ask:

- What is a hero? Focus on all heroes, not just superheroes. (Ordinary people who do extraordinary things?)
- How can someone act like a hero – what does heroism mean to you? (Doing good, being the first to help, putting the needs of others first?)
- What do heroes have in common? (Amazing at what they do? Help us? Brave? Overcome problems?)
- Do you have any heroes?
- How can we be kind hearted and caring heroes to our friends?

Case study – what is a hero? Out of the mouths of babes!

"Someone who does super good stuff!" Edgar, aged four and three-quarters

"A hero is someone who has a heart and wings!" Grace, aged 4

"Superheroes have superpowers!" James, aged 4

"Someone who saves the goodies from the baddies. They fight the baddies!" Dylan, aged 4

"I'm not sure what a hero is, but I know we dressed up as superheroes for the New Year's Eve party. But I've only seen them on TV. I will ask Edward (big brother) what an actual hero is!" Emily, aged 4

"I've drawn Daddy. He is my hero" Amelia, aged 4.

Case study – superhero writing

Tom (five years two months) wanted to write a note to his daddy and he wrote this, it says:

"To dad

Soopu Hirow (superhero)

luve (love)

Tom"

He told his dad that the crosses are kisses.

A heart-warming story has recently hit the headlines in the UK about a young person who felt so devastated that a bridge near her home was often a popular spot for those wanting to end their lives that she wrote notes and pinned them to the bridge. The police believe that this small act of kindness has saved many lives. This is what being an everyday hero is about – shining a light in the darkness, enabling others to carry on, believe in themselves or achieve great things. My friend was reminded of this recently when she wanted to give up on a task that she found difficult. Her five-year-old son chastised her saying: "That's not being a St Mary's learner Mummy! We try and try again!" He is receiving these messages from school and had transferred them into his home life with his Mummy.

There are, of course, more momentous occasions when children have saved the day, for example, phoning paramedics if their parent had an accident or waking up the household and escaping when a fire broke out. These occasions can be shared with children and we can teach them skills such as how to call the emergency services. Some children can become worried or anxious about potential dangers, so it is important to know our children really well and to remain sensitive to their needs while teaching them these life-saving skills.

We also need to teach children about small acts that are also heroic in their own way and might make a big difference for someone else. For example, asking someone to play with you if they are on their own or smiling at someone who feels very sad and asking if you can help. These everyday acts of kindness can make a huge difference to someone's day and even their life!

Case study – acts of kindness

A Church of England primary school invited children to participate in a scheme at particular points in their religious year. Rather than give up something for Lent, children were encouraged to promise to do something kind and during Advent, as a run-up to Christmas, children were invited to undertake at least one act of kindness each day. The sorts of kind act they listed include:

- Give away a toy to charity
- Help your parent around the home
- Smile at someone
- Make a card for a friend
- Play with someone who is on their own
- Hold a door open for someone

These events are an opportunity to talk to children about being kind, being a good friend and what this means.

Another key message that we want our children to hear is that heroes come in all shapes and sizes – men, women, boys, girls, all nationalities, all ethnic groups, all socioeconomic statuses and so on. Everyone can be a hero when they show compassion or care for others. The US Department of Education (2018) states: "Heroes are everywhere and sharing stories about them can help children understand what qualities it takes to be a hero and what heroism really means."

We need to instil in our children the qualities that they recognise in the people they look up to, in order for them to become adults who are resilient, hard working, have inner strength, steadfastness and can persevere when the going gets tough. Chapter 10 explores this further in terms of how we can encourage children to find their own superpowers.

Case study – Westview Day Nursery

At Westview, we regularly focus on people who help us and everyday heroes and invite visitors into our setting to talk to the children about what they do. In addition, whenever possible we follow up on children's interests and we recently had one child who was particularly interested in crime and the police. This led to us setting up a provocation in the outdoor area, like a crime scene, in which Humpty Dumpty had fallen off his wall. The police were called and they had to investigate if he had fallen or whether he had been pushed! The officers fully entered into the spirit of the investigation and the children loved being interviewed and talking to the officers. Throughout this play episode, the children found out a lot about what the police do, how they help us and what to do in an emergency.

Playing at being a hero

In addition to real-life people who we look up to, children also celebrate heroism by regularly recreating events and situations that they have experienced, often taking on character roles and imitating grownups. This social and dramatic play, or sociodramatic play as it can be referred to, usually happens within the free-play element of a session and tends to be child led. We see it emerging when children begin to engage socially with each other at around two and a half to three years old, however, it is not until around age four or five that their play becomes more involved with complicated themes. It is a social and cooperative enterprise that often develops through collaboration with others and is linked to the children's interests and real-life experiences.

Although children regularly initiate this play, we can still influence, plan and very occasionally direct it when we feel it is appropriate to do so. We must be careful to ensure we are "interacting not interfering" (Fisher, 2016). Many a time I have attempted to join a group of children in their play, only to find that the play stops and I am surplus to requirements! Therefore, we need to observe children's play, assess whether to continue observing or whether to intervene sensitively.

Children need time, space and access to resources to develop their play themes. However, we do not need to resource every element of their play. In doing so, we would remove the opportunity for them to draw on their imagination and engage in symbolic play, pretending an object is something else. The best resources that we can provide children are real objects, as opposed to pretend ones or open-ended resources that can be used in a variety of ways. Think about it: a real pumpkin is immensely different from a plastic one and pieces of material can be transformed into a tent one day and a cape the next. We may like to add a few resources and props to assist with specific roles, e.g. a doctor's kit or a label saying campsite … Remember that the more you are able to involve children in this process the more successful it will be; if the idea is theirs and they talk about the objects and props needed, how they can be used and help to mark make and create signs and symbols to enhance the area, then the more engaged the children will be in their play.

We can widen children's experiences by offering them opportunities to find out more about a role once they have shown an interest. For example, if a child has just visited a dentist and begins to play at dentists with their friend, we could arrange to visit a dentist's surgery or invite a dentist to visit us so that we can find out more about this role. Perhaps we can involve the children in creating a dental surgery in an area of our room.

Sometimes we can just stand back and watch the drama unfold. It might be in a specific area (e.g. role-play area/construction area) or it could develop in any space that the children occupy, inside or outside. It is important to value this play wherever it appears, as it is through playing in this way that children are learning how to act and behave in their world. There are many other noted benefits for children engaging in social and dramatic play. It:

- Develops children's self-regulation skills.
- Enhances and practises their language and communication skills.
- Provides an opportunity to interact socially.
- Helps children to understand the world and how it works.
- Develops children's understanding of rules and social etiquette.
- Allows children to be creative and use their imagination.

- Provides opportunities to use literacy skills.
- Practises using long- and short-term memory.
- Develops children's ability to problem solve and think critically.

If children are already engaging in social and dramatic play successfully, we probably do not need to intervene at all; however, through observing children we may want to enrich their play by introducing new props, role modelling, extending the narrative, sharing vocabulary relating to the play theme or offering ideas to extend their play. We have two options when it comes to joining in: we can interact without participating or become a participant. If we remain outside the play we might intervene by asking questions, e.g. "What are you going to cook?" or commenting on the play "Put the doctor's stethoscope around your neck and listen to their heartbeat ..." We are acknowledging the play taking place and addressing the character they are portraying, rather than interrupting the play and addressing the child. Brown et al. (undated) talk about children as being constant method actors in the way that they take on roles in their play and become the character themselves and intervening by addressing them as the character values their acting ability.

The other option is to participate and take on a role in the play. In an ideal world, you would be invited in to join the play by the children themselves, however, if you are not, you may try to sensitively take on a character and role model how to be a "baker" or a "police officer". This is a particularly useful strategy if children need support to fully understand the role that they are taking on. However, the best way for them to fully understand a role is for them to have first-hand experience of it, so take the children on outings, invite visitors into your settings and bring in resources and artefacts to bring sociodramatic play to life.

Case study – Westview Day Nursery

We invited firefighters to visit our setting and they arrived with the fire engine much to the delight of the children. We found out about how firefighters help people and had a go at using the fire hose!

After this visit, the children engaged in lots of dramatic play around firefighters and we made resources and props to enhance their play.

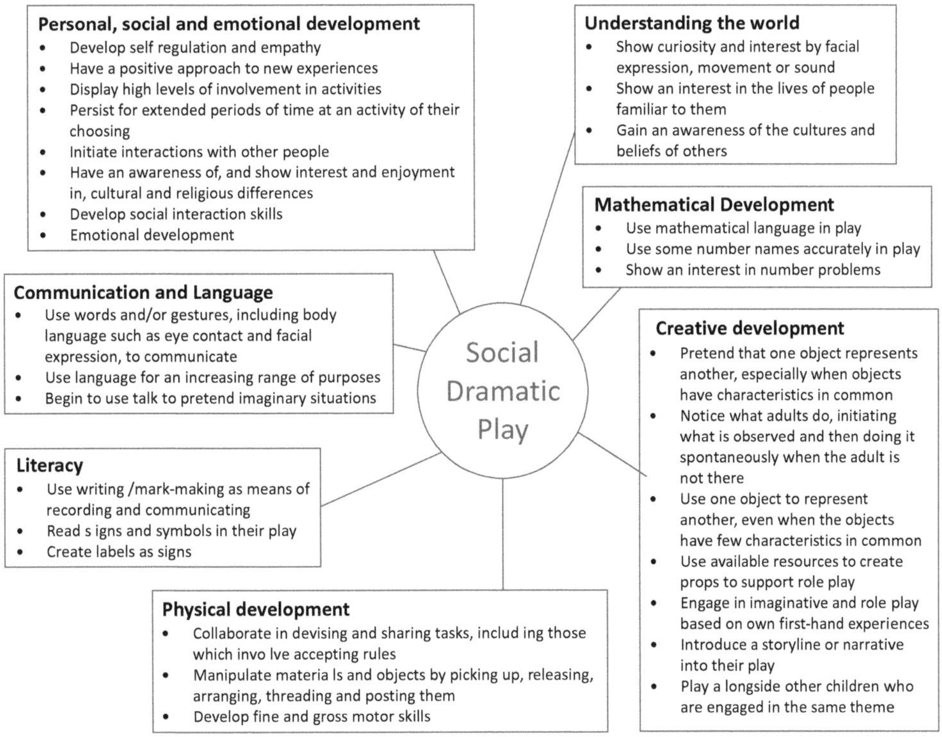

Figure 6.6 Linking Social and dramatic play to areas of learning in the Early Years Foundation Stage.

Sociodramatic play is classified as the most highly developed form of symbolic play (Frost and Klein, 1979) and builds on children's basic symbolic play, as described by Piaget, when objects stand for other objects in their play (1954). One example of this was when a child picked up a wooden block and swiped it with his index finger, stating that he was just checking his emails! Vygotsky talked a lot about play and its importance in helping children to develop self-regulation skills: "In play a child behaves beyond his average age, above his daily behaviour; in play it is as though he were a head taller than himself" (Vygotsky, 1978, p. 102). Figure 6.6 shows how social and dramatic play can support children in all areas of learning and development.

The bystander effect

It could be argued that the nemesis of real-life heroes is the bystander effect. This is the idea that whether or not you will help in an emergency situation depends on the number of people present at the time. This has also been linked to bullying within educational establishments and whether or not an individual will intervene in a group situation when another child is being bullied. Many people assume that bullying does not happen within early childhood settings, due to the young age of the children involved. Sadly, this is not always the case and there is a wealth of evidence to suggest that bullying can begin at a very young age, usually between three and six years (Kirves & Sajaniemi, 2012; Repo and Sajaniemi, 2015).

Bullying could be defined as an occasion when an individual is repeatedly aggressive towards, or deliberately tries to hurt or cause distress to, another individual. This is usually linked to an imbalance when the bully dominates the victim and the victim struggles to defend themselves. As Chapter 2 discusses, aggressive play is a normal type of interaction that many children engage in and thus it is important to distinguish between bullying and aggressive play. When a child is deliberately aggressive towards a specific child and this happens on a regular basis, we would need to ascertain whether they are meaning to cause harm and therefore are acting with real intent to hurt. Many aggressive behaviours in early childhood are actually a result of frustration or an impulsive response, for example, I feel angry so I am lashing out. For bullying to be deemed as taking place, the child who is being aggressive needs to want to harm the other child and so lashing out in anger or frustration doesn't fit this description. Children also need to have an understanding that other people feel and can hurt, which links in with our theory of mind discussion earlier in this chapter.

Case study – a parent's perspective

When Sarah, my middle child, was aged between 18 months and three and a half years, she went through a phase of hurting other children. Prior to this age she would spend most of her time watching others playing and playing on her own. Sarah would go up to another child, then reach out and grab her face. This would clearly hurt the other child and once, I remember with horror, she even drew blood. I would have to try to shadow her, chasing her around the various toddler groups watching for signs that she was about to strike! This was particularly difficult as I often had her siblings with me and would need to be feeding the baby or chasing her older sister. There didn't appear to be any pattern and it certainly didn't happen when she was upset or angry; if anything she appeared to hurt others more frequently when she was happy! Over time, I began to realise that she was actually wanting to play with these children and was reaching and grabbing their faces out of a desire to interact. Although Sarah had a good grasp of language, she didn't appear to know how to begin playing with other children.

I remember this phase was a really difficult time for me as her Mum, as there is such a stigma attached to children who hurt others and other parents began to give me horrified looks when we arrived at groups. Thankfully, I often attended groups with friends who knew Sarah and how delightful she could be; they also sympathised with my difficulty in having my three children with me and would keep an eye on Sarah when I needed to feed or change her younger sister's nappy.

When Sarah was about six we referred her via our doctor because we suspected that she was on the autistic spectrum. Although it took nearly three years of waiting for the diagnosis, she was eventually diagnosed as having ASD (autistic spectrum disorder) when she had just turned nine. During these years, we noticed that when Sarah wanted to play with someone else or when she particularly liked another child, she would poke them, kiss them or play with their shoes or hair. Looking back, I realise that grabbing children's faces was her way of saying: "I want to play with you!"

Occasionally, as in the case study above, aggression may be a sign of an emotional issue or an undiagnosed learning difficulty. In the light of this and our uncertainty relating to young children's real intent to harm, we must express caution in labelling a child as a bully at a very young age. Repo and Sajaniemi (2015) ask educators to express caution when using the word "bully" with young children as they argue that it can cause stigmatisation of either the bully or the victim. However, they do highlight the importance of addressing the issue and putting preventative measures into place. One way to do this is to teach children how to speak out and be the first to respond. Staub, who has conducted a considerable amount of work in this field, defines bystanders as: "People who are in a position to know what is happening and in a position to take action" (2005, p. 97). In one research project, he found that if a child had been told not to go into a certain room and then distress sounds were coming from that room, the child were less likely to go in. If they had been given permission to go into that room, for example, to get more pencils, they would help 90% of the time, but if they had not been explicitly given permission or had been prohibited from going into the room, they acted as if they had been prohibited and were less likely to go in (Staub, 2018). This is interesting and possibly demonstrates the importance of rules and boundaries with young children. Perhaps we also need to explain to children that there may be are times when we can bend, or even break, the rules to help someone else. Some of our everyday heroes have done just that, for example, a firefighter might need to break a window to allow a person to escape from a burning building.

Some studies have found that young children did not readily show the bystander effect, as they are more likely to help than older children regardless of whether they are alone or part of a group, however, Staub found that some children actually help more when they are able to talk to others about the situation and when they have more opportunities to practise being helpful (2018). He refers to "active bystandership" and how being a bystander presents people with an opportunity to act positively. This has implications for us in our settings as we can foster helpfulness and link this in with being a real hero ourselves.

Ways in which to counter the bystander effect and become active bystanders are listed below:

- Use social stories which show how other people think and feel in different situations.
- Ask the children how they know if someone needs our help and talk about being helpers.
- Offer children plenty of opportunities to be "helpers" in the setting and to help and care for others.
- Share stories with alternate endings and discuss with children which was the kindest response.
- Use puppets and share a narrative that involves a bully and the puppet witnessing bullying. What should the puppet do?
- Plan role-play scenarios that present children with choices of how to act and what to do.
- Talk about being the first to respond, being the first to act and how it feels to be the first to do something differently from their friends.
- Celebrate difference and diversity and instil the ethos that it's OK to be yourself, even if this is different from others.
- Share stories where doing nothing was the wrong choice and being apathetic caused more harm than good.
- Talk about defending other people or defending those who are not able to defend themselves, e.g. pets, wildlife etc.
- Use conflict resolution techniques such as the problem-solving approach outlined in Chapter 8 to address potential bullying and remain non-judgemental.
- Support children's self-regulation skills and actively promote their understanding of theory of mind.

Observing children's play

It can be helpful to reflect on children's play that we regularly observe. They may incorporate elements of fantasy and reality into their play as discussed in Chapter 1. We can find out about children's experiences and interests in relation to real-life heroes through our observations and then plan to incorporate these interests into future sessions. We might want to find books to support their interests and include these in the book area, as well as provide the children with opportunities to further explore these ideas.

You may find the following questions insightful:

- How did the children decide what to play?
- How did children involve other children or adults in their play?
- How did the invited child or adult indicate they wanted to join in?
- How did children create boundaries around their play?
- In what ways did the play incorporate elements of both fantasy and reality?
- Did children use objects or props in this play? If so, how were these objects used?
- To what extent did the play involve verbal communication?
- Did the play theme change or adapt? If so, how?
- How did the children end the play activity?
- How long did the play sustain and how would you describe the children's levels of involvement and engagement during the play episode?

Case study – reception class building site

Several children demonstrated an interest in building sites and construction so the reception team decided to create an outside role play area where children could re-enact this play.

Builders are really important heroes because without them our houses would fall down!

There are plenty of opportunities to play with the concept of real-life heroes. Here are some ideas of how to promote this play in your setting:

- Follow the children's lead and allow them to plan areas, gather resources, imagine things and improvise.
- Provide artefacts or props and encourage the children to create their own props, labels and signs to enhance their play.
- Offer opportunities for role play inside and outside.
- Invite visitors into your setting who could be described as heroes, for example, fire-fighters, park rangers or police officers. Ask them to explain their daily activities, equipment, training and why they enjoy their jobs.
- Plan an event with the children that encourages them to be heroes, too – for example a sponsored walk that raises money for charity or helping to remove plastic from the local beach or visiting a residential care home for the elderly.
- Show the children the various icons and logos that many heroes have and create a logo for an everyday hero of their choice.
- Encourage the children to make "My Hero!" cards for someone in their family who has inspired them.
- Show children newspaper cuttings of heroes and heroic acts – courage or service to community.
- Show children pictures of figures living and dead who have been called heroes – choose people you admire …
- Notice and encourage kindness, for example, through creating a kindness jar or promoting acts of kindness at specific times of year.
- Encourage children to be involved in community projects, serving others in some way, for example, collecting food for the local food bank.
- Read stories and rhymes to the children that focus on heroism and overcoming difficulties.
- Create a display about "Our Heroes" to celebrate everyday heroism.
- Provide opportunities for children to become heroes themselves (see Chapter 10).

In summary

Children will often have real people in their lives they are in awe of. This might be an older sibling, their parent, an authority figure or community member. They may also have heard stories about ordinary people who do extraordinary things and are everyday heroes. We can talk to children about these people and encourage them to further explore heroism through play and discussion.

Very young children do not understand that other people think and feel differently from us and will often act on impulse. We need to plan activities and offer opportunities that support children to develop theory of mind and self-regulation. They will then have the skills and understanding needed in order to truly celebrate difference, become helpers rather than bystanders and have the strength of character required to recognise the call and become heroes themselves.

Questions for reflection

1 How can you share stories about everyday heroism with your children?
2 Who do the children in your setting look up to and in what ways can you incorporate their heroes into play opportunities?
3 What opportunities can you provide for children to practise being kind and helpful?

References

Brown, P., Sutterby, J., Therrell, J. and Thornton, C. (undated) The importance of free play to children's development. Retrieved from http://www.imaginationplayground.com/images/content/3/0/3001/The-Importance-of-Free-Play-to-Children-s-Development.doc

Department for Education (DfE) (2017) Statutory framework for the early years foundation stage. Retrieved from http://www.foundationyears.org.uk/eyfs-statutory-framework/

Evans, A. D. and Lee, K. (2013) Emergence of lying in very young children, *Developmental Psychology*, *49*(10), pp. 1958–1963

Fisher, J. (2016) *Interacting or Interfering?* London: Open University Press

Frost, J. and Klein, B. (1979) *Children's Play and Playgrounds*. Boston, MA: Allyn & Bacon

German, T. and Leslie, A. (2001) Children's inferences from "knowing" to "pretending" and "believing", *British Journal of Developmental Psychology*, *19*, pp. 59–83

Harris, K. I. (2016) Heroes of resiliency and reciprocity: teachers' supporting role for reconceptualizing superhero play in early childhood settings, *Pastoral Care in Education*, *34*(4), pp. 202–217

Kirves, L. and Sajaniemi, N. (2012) Bullying in early educational settings, *Early Child Development and Care*, *182* (3–4), pp. 383–400

Piaget, J. (1954) *The Construction of Reality in the Child*. Abingdon: Routledge & Kegan Paul.

Repo, L. and Sajaniemi, N. (2015) Bystanders' roles and children with special educational needs in bullying situations among preschool-aged children, *Early Years*, *35*(1), pp. 5–21

Staub, E. (2005) The roots of goodness: the fulfilment of basic human needs and the development of caring, helping and nonaggression, inclusive caring, moral courage, active bystandership, and altruism born of suffering. In Carlo, G. Edwards, C. (Eds.) *Moral Motivation through the Life Span: Theory, Research, Applications*. Nebraska Symposium on Motivation. Lincoln, NE: Nebraska University Press

Staub, E. (2018) Preventing violence and promoting active bystandership and peace: my life in research and applications, *Peace and Conflict: Journal of Peace Psychology*, *24*(1), pp. 95–111

Talwar, V. and Lee, K. (2008) Social and cognitive correlates of children's lying behavior, *Child Development*, (4), p. 866US Department of Education (2018) Activities III – helping your child become a responsible citizen. Retrieved from https://www2.ed.gov/parents/academic/help/citizen/part9.html

Vygotsky, L. S. (1978) *Mind in Society: The Development of Higher Mental Processes*. Cambridge, MA: Harvard University Press.

7 "Where's my cape?"

Creating a super learning environment

Introduction

Getting the learning environment right is an essential component of an effective early years setting. One of the principles of the Early Years Foundation Stage in the United Kingdom is that: "Children learn and develop well in enabling environments, in which their experiences respond to their individual needs and there is a strong partnership between practitioners and parents and/or carers" (Department for Education (DfE), 2017, p. 6). This is talking about using what you know about the children as your starting point and responding sensitively to them, so observing the children and using this knowledge to plan an interesting and exciting environment that is both safe and stimulating. For activities to work well, link them to your children's first-hand experiences and interests and be ready to role model, extend learning or continue observing as appropriate.

Most settings have children who have an interest in popular culture and superhero play so this is a good place to start. You can use characters from these games or themes that emerge from their play as a hook to get children engrossed in what you offer. You may have come across the term provocation meaning when adults present children with interesting and thought-provoking ideas and environments for them to investigate and explore. I like to think about them as "invitations to play" and an example of this was when the educators at St Mary's School prepared large dinosaur footprints in the playground for the children to discover (see Chapter 1).

In the image above, the small world resources were presented in such a way that they invite the child in to continue the narrative suggested by the characters.

Consider your approach

It might be helpful to think about your learning environment as mirroring your ethos around how young children should learn. For example, if you believe that children need to become independent and autonomous in their learning, your environment should have low-level, accessible resources that the children can access independently or, if you want to encourage a love of reading, you need to ensure that children see you reading, you read to children, you have an exciting book area and books and print can be found in all areas of your setting.

Papatheodorou argues that: "Learning environments are socially constructed: the learning environments we create in early years settings are influenced by our beliefs and values and the relevant theoretical models we embrace" (2010, p. 145). Odstock Day Nursery is an example of a setting whose learning environment is totally influenced by the values it upholds. It is inspired by practices such as those in Reggio Emilia (explored later in this chapter) and views children as competent learners who have a natural inclination to discover and it presents its learning environment in the light of this. Adults present children with provocations that they can explore and offer them access to a wealth of different open-ended materials. They have also found that this freedom leads to fewer disagreements over resources and more cooperation and collaboration.

Case study – open-ended resources and loose-parts play at Odstock Day Nursery

The children at Odstock Day Nursery are able to engage with the open-ended resources and decide what to create in whichever way they want to. The educators supporting them understand the importance of allowing children to lead their own learning and respectfully offer time and space for children to develop their own creations. On this occasion, the children wanted to make a Christmas tree and spent a long time collaborating and working out how to create a star and then attach it to the top.

One aspect of the environment that you will want to consider is to ensure that your practice is as inclusive as possible. This will not only be about having a positive ethos so that every child feels included, but also that you offer accessible resources and equal access to activities. Think about the needs of your children in your group. The youngest children may need resources to be at floor level to enable them to reach and some children may need to have a quiet space to retreat to when things get a little overwhelming. Your resources should reflect different cultures in your local community and you need to ensure that you have a range of strong powerful female superheroes as well as more traditional Batman types. A great toy that I have discovered is the Lottie Doll. She is Barbie sized but her body is designed to the proportions of a young girl, rather than those of an inaccurate woman! She is pictured in her superhero costume in the photograph in the introduction.

If your environment is truly inclusive, it will ensure that no child or family is disadvantaged because of factors such as background, ethnicity, faith or disability etc. Think about equity and equality of opportunity for the children and families in your setting. I was reminded of this recently when I saw a poster of an adult and two children of differing heights trying to watch a ball game over a tall wooden fence (Xiong, 2017). The poster had three different scenarios: the first showed them all standing on a box. The adult is now really tall and the children can all see, but trying to overcome the difficulty by treating everyone equally is crazy in this scenario. The second picture shows the children standing on one box or two in order to even out their heights, which has enabled everyone to see and thus demonstrates being treated equitably. However, the third image shows that simply changing the wooden fence to a wire barrier that they can all see through actually removes the cause of the inequality in the first place. Sometimes we need to look at things from a different angle to be truly inclusive.

Learning from past educators

When it comes to play-based learning and creating learning environments for our superheroes we can learn from the wealth of educationalists who have preceded us. Take the McMillan sisters as an example: they were promoting outdoor learning through playback in the late 19th century alongside Isaacs who discouraged the desk-based learning that was so prevalent in schools at this time (Pound, 2005). About 100 years earlier, Froebel famously coined the term "kindergarten" for his institute for play and activity for small children. This literally means "children's garden" and the children attending engaged in early learning experiences such as free play and outdoor learning (Pound, 2005).

Montessori also viewed the environment as incredibly important for learning. She believed that adults should build an environment designed specifically for children, so that "the child can live in a state of beauty" (1936, p.260). She insisted on child-sized furniture so that children could be as independent as possible, an idea that all modern settings embrace. Nowadays tables and chairs tend to be the correct size for the children who occupy them and we often purchase all sorts of mini-versions of adult tools from irons to lawnmowers.

It could be argued that, in the past, many classrooms were deliberately designed with desks in rows to fit lots of children into the room and to limit movement as much as possible! Some of us have inherited Victorian classrooms or village halls to work in and it is very difficult to engage in superhero play when there is very little space to play! We need to think about the physical layout of our play-space. I would argue that children under five do not all need to be sitting on a chair at the same time. If they are, I would question how many opportunities they have for physical and active learning. Even in a reception class serving four- and five-year-olds, educators should organise the environment and routine to minimise time spent being inactive and sitting at desks. We can learn from others who have thought carefully about how the physical environment impacts on the learning climate.

Several years ago I was lucky enough to visit Reggio Emilia in northern Italy while on a UK study tour. The kindergartens and infant-toddler centres in this town are world leaders in terms of their excellent early years practice. The main aspects of their practice that others try to replicate are the stunning environments that are created and the way that children are encouraged to lead their own learning. In Reggio, the environment is so highly regarded and important that it is viewed as the "third teacher" with most educational settings having two teachers, the *pedagogista* who is the main educator and the *atelierista* who works as a creative lead or artist in the setting (Edwards, Gandini and Foreman, 2012). The space in which the children work is seen as in itself educating the child, in terms of the resources available, their accessibility, how flexibly the space and resources can be used and how it mirrors the children who occupy it. Educators spend a great deal of time planning how space will be used and displaying resources beautifully. The photograph shows an aesthetically beautiful craft or collage area that the children were free to access with items ordered in shades of colour and mirrors placed behind the resources. It is inviting and puts many of my attempts at providing accessible resources to shame!

Although the way we present resources can help to provide a stimulating environment, Vygotsky (1978) would argue that the social aspects of learning are vitally important as the case study about the Power Rangers training camp just demonstrated. Children do not learn in isolation and we can offer them many opportunities to learn with their peers as well as with educators. Superhero play offers a perfect context for social learning such as this.

Case study – Power Ranger training camp!

Most of the year, Power Rangers were the favourite superheroes for a group of children at St Mary's Preschool. At forest school sessions the children would find sticks to be weapons so we helped to make them better weapons, creating their own bows and arrows, of which made the children were immensely proud.

We also decided to have a Power Ranger training camp to ensure our Power Rangers were fit for the job of saving the planet. We made a base to start with, using a tarpaulin and putting up a tent. Children needed to learn to put the tent pegs in and to tie knots. This really helped with children's fine motor control and involved collaboration as one child needed to hold the tarp while the other pegged it in.

The children bounced ideas off one another when deciding how to design and make their training course.

The final course offered opportunities to balance, go under and over obstacles and finished with a slackline.

At the end of the session the Power Rangers were feeling fit and they decided that their mission was to dig for chocolate coins for the teachers (sounded good to us!) in another area. They worked amazingly hard at this, encouraging one another to keep going. One child said: "Children never give up!"

Lastly, the children decided that we needed a sign to tell everyone that this was the training camp. So I role modelled writing the letters on some bark in charcoal, telling the children each sound as I did so and the children enjoyed tracing over them in chalk.

Incorporating mindfulness

It is also important, however, for children to have time to calm down in addition to time playing with others at full speed! Mindfulness is a popular concept at present; you could even call it a craze in itself, however, it is vitally important that in our busy lives we take time out to reflect on what we do and calm down. Superhero play may not sound very compatible with being mindful, however, physical play is one way that children feel grounded and in the moment and certainly in touch with their senses, which are all concepts woven throughout mindfulness.

We can explain to children that there were times when all superheroes needed to relax, recharge their batteries or simply sleep. Not even heroes can run on empty! Practising mindfulness can also help children to develop self-regulation and respond to events in proportion to what has happened. Young children find it difficult to control their emotions and superhero play is an ideal context in which to support them to do this. Chapter 3 explores some strategies to enable children to become more emotionally literate such as emotion coaching.

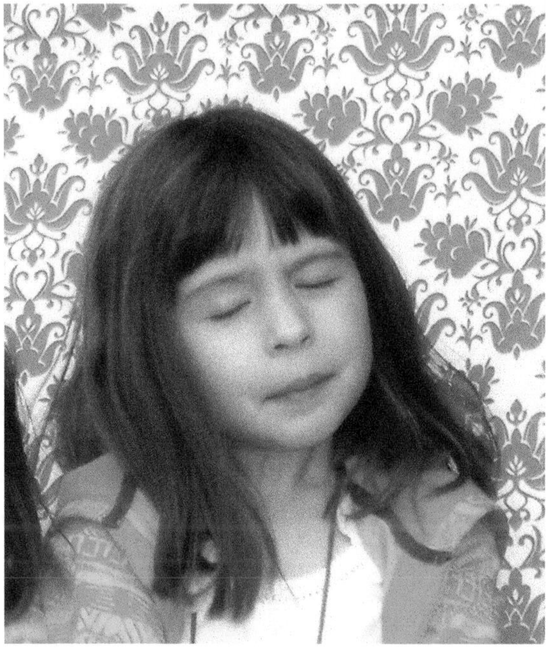

When practising mindfulness, encourage children to shut their eyes and engage their senses, what can they hear, smell, feel and so on. This is called grounding, when we try to take stock of the here and now, noticing our body regardless of what is going on around us. We can also name our feelings and acknowledge them as this is a powerful way to feel more at ease with how we feel. There are numerous websites, instruction books and videos that can help us to practise mindfulness. I have included one idea below based on Spider-Man that you might like to try with your children to increase their focus.

Case study – Spider-Man meditation

You may like to try this Spider-Man meditation with your children to practise mindfulness. It was written by Zemirah Jazwierska (2003) and shared on the kids' relaxation website (www.kidsrelaxation.com). Prepare for the activity by gathering the resources that are needed and then slowly read through the script below.

Materials needed: bell, flowers, small food item (such as a raspberry or a raisin). Please feel free to use whatever small food you like suitable for the age of children you are working with. Remember to check with parents about any allergies prior to this activity.

One of Spider-Man's superpowers was the ability to tune into his senses. Like a spider, he could hear very tiny noises. He was able to pay very close attention to the noises. When you pay very close attention, you are able to calm your mind and let go of all the noisy thoughts in your head that can be distracting. With practise, you can improve your focus and relax right now, right where you are.

Right now we are going to learn to activate your superpowers to tune into your senses, just like Spider-Man. These are your Spider-Man Super Senses. What it takes is a little practise. Let's start with your sense of hearing. First let's sit down. Close your eyes and place your hands on your knees. I am going to ring a bell. When you hear the bell, pay attention to the ring until you can no longer hear the ringing sound, clasp your hands together in your lap. (Repeat 3 times). Like Spider-Man, we have activated your super power of ultra hearing! Excellent work!

Next we are going to activate your superpowers of ultra seeing, touching and smelling. I'm going to give each of you a flower. Hold your flower gently in your hand. When I ring the bell, I want you to gently touch the petals. Feel what each petal is like beneath your fingers. Pay attention to whether the petal is soft, rough, wet, furry, smooth, or prickly. See what you can feel. Imagine, like Spider-Man, your hands have the power to sense very carefully what the flower feels like. As I ring the bell next, I want you to smell the flower. Breathe in deeply with the flower under your nose. See what the flower's scent is. Is it sweet? Maybe it has very little smell at all? What do you smell? Now, finally, as I ring the bell, I want you to look very closely at the flower. Pay attention to the lines on the petals. What does the centre of the flower look like? Is it bumpy? Smooth? Soft looking? Wet looking? Is there powdery pollen in the centre? See what details you can notice in the flower, what little shapes, what lines, what circles, if any. (Ring the bell a final time to signal the end of the activity).

The final activation of your Spider-Man super power of ultra senses, is to practise your sense of taste. We are going to practise by tasting, paying very close attention to what a raspberry/raisin tastes like. Start by looking at the berry and noticing, using your super power sight, what the berry looks like. Turn the berry gently between your fingers, feeling what the berry feels like. Next, place the berry in your mouth. Keep the berry in your mouth, paying attention to how it feels on your tongue and how the juices in your mouth start to flow. Now slowly begin to chew the berry. See how slowly you can chew it. How does it taste? Sweet? Tart? Sour? Gently swallow the berry, paying attention to the taste that remains in your mouth after you swallow it.

Now you have activated all of your Spider-Man Super Senses! Remember that when you are very quiet and focus, your body and mind are able to relax and take a break from the day's busy activities. You have the power to activate your Spider-Man Super Senses whenever you want to calm down and focus for a moment.

A rich learning environment that supports superhero play

The great thing about superhero play is that you don't need to invest in expensive equipment or special costumes. There are plenty of superhero resources available to buy if you choose to, however, I don't think that this always enhances their play. Providing children with loose parts and open-ended resources will allow them to create their own superhero environments. For example, you could follow up on a child's interest in Batman and create a bat cave by draping a large piece of dark material over a table. Add a few ultra-violet pens and torches and it becomes incredibly inviting! Children can then draw their own logos or educators can print images to decorate the cave … Sticking a bat shape to a torch makes a great bat signal and a Batman utility belt can easily be created if you provide children with long pieces of yellow or gold card or material. Children will come up with their own ideas and all educators need to do is ensure that there are accessible materials available.

In addition, although there is sometimes a place for ready-made costumes e.g. Spider-Man outfit, or Batman mask, providing children with open-ended materials and non-hero-specific costumes will enable them to develop their play in their own way. Sometimes a Spider-Man outfit can be restrictive, for example, a child may feel that they can *only* be Spider-Man in that outfit. What if they are playing a game when they want to fly? Spider-Man can't fly and this outfit will restrict their play. Offering children generic capes, large pieces of material or non-specific eye masks can open up their play to many more opportunities. You may like to make superhero capes with your children. Perhaps make less traditional ones too, like Widcombe Acorns did, for example, a flowery cape or a pink-lined cape, as well as blue, red and black.

We cannot and should not provide resources for every possible scenario or scene. This would remove the opportunity for children to use their own imagination and to improvise with resources. Also, we don't know what our children will be interested in and which ideas they will want to take forward so we could even be wasting our time. Too many resources could actually change an open-ended activity into a closed one.

Case study – Widcombe Acorns

This preschool made children a selection of generic capes that the children could use to become their own superheroes. They wanted to leave this as open ended as possible to enable children to use their own ideas, creativity and imagination about the superpowers and skillsets of the hero they became. They also ensured that they used a real mix of material to create them from pink and flowery to star studded. The capes were a huge success and helped the children's storylines to extend and develop away from simply "I'm Spider-Man" or "I'm Superman!"

Opportunities to learn

We can use superhero play in its broadest sense to help children to learn in a number of different areas. In addition to the ideas contained in other chapters in this book, I have listed below a few thoughts on how to link these themes with different areas of learning or development. I have broadly based these areas of learning on those in the Early Years Foundation Stage (DfE, 2017), however, I have tweaked the areas slightly to widen their range.

Communication and language, reading and writing:

- Superhero stories and rhymes
- A super writing area and inviting book area
- Secret writing: invisible inks, UV pens, pencil on black paper and torches, white chalk or crayon on white paper
- Helicopter stories (Lee, 2016)
- Story stones or superhero gemstones
- Mark making and writing labels, signs and logos
- Writing captions and creating cartoon storyboards

- Superhero story sacks
- Recognising logos.

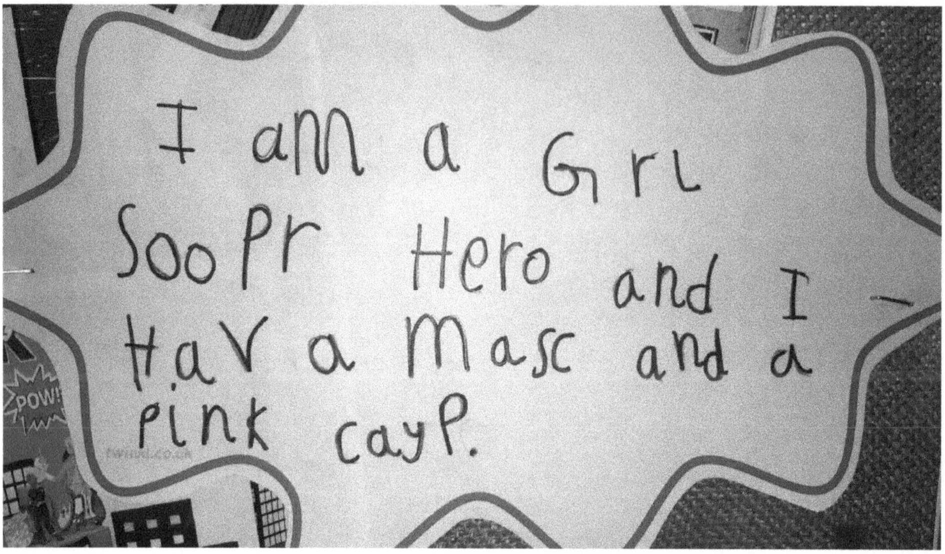

Case study – Supertato to the rescue!

A reception class read a story about a superhero called Supertato and wrote their own Supertato story. They then created their own vegetable characters and wrote captions for them. The children loved the story and it gave them incentive to write for a purpose.

Their work was then displayed on the wall and shared with parents.

Physical development, fine and gross motor skills:

- Rough and tumble play
- Staged fight scenes
- Superhero training camp and obstacle course
- Building camps, tying knots when den building
- Whittling sticks to become swords
- Superhero jigsaws and puzzles
- Opening padlocks to release captives
- Mission impossible-type mazes made with wool.

Case study – making lightsabers

During a phase when lots of children were interested in Star Wars, these children whittled a stick with a potato peeler to strip off the bark. They then created their own lightsabers to use in their fantasy play.

Personal, social and emotional development and wellbeing:

- Thinking about goodies and baddies
- Staying safe – who can we turn to when we're in trouble?
- Exploring concepts around killing and death
- Mindfulness and meditation
- Circle time – becoming an everyday hero
- Role play
- Conflict resolution
- What would your super powers be?

Case study – superhero licence

One setting had a group of children who were very into superhero play one year and found that children were regularly play fighting with each other. They explored what superheroes do and focused on the way they are strong, protect the weak and help (not hurt) others. In the light of this, the educators and children drew up some superhero rules for everyone to keep during the sessions. These rules were designed to remind the children when play fighting not to hurt one another as well as to limit behaviour such as running inside their setting. They created a poster reminding children and adults alike of the rules and at the end of each week held a special ceremony when the children engaging in superhero play dressed in their costumes and were thanked for keeping their superhero rules and keeping everyone safe. They created licences, which they presented to the children during this ceremony. This continued for several weeks until the children naturally lost interest.

- Create superhero ID cards
- Discuss rules and boundaries.

Mathematical development:

- Web patterns
- Logo shapes and patterns
- Problem solving
- Superhero gemstone counters
- Counting, numbers of heroes and villains, windows on skyscrapers
- Exploring safe combinations.

Case study – Spider-Man's web

Children in a reception class were recognising, creating and describing patterns within their mathematics lessons. They looked at webs in the natural world, then created their own webs out of string tied around a hoop. This not only developed their fine motor skills but also their understanding of patterns in the environment.

Scientific understanding of the natural world and its people:

- Exploring our super senses
- Find out about real-life heroes
- Small world play with superhero characters
- Sociodramatic play around real-life heroes
- Exploring light and dark in a bat cave with torches.

Case study – super secret bat writing!

A childminding setting created a bat cave out of a clothes horse and a black sheet. The children were given several torches and lights and explored light and dark inside the "cave". They also had the opportunity to try "secret" writing, which the children found very exciting. The childminder had cut several pieces of black card into bat shapes and left some HB pencils in the cave. When written on they are difficult to read unless you shine a torch on them, hence secret writing! It was a super success!

Case study – Ghostbuster slime at St Mary's Preschool

Several children went through a phase of playing Ghostbusters. On one occasion, two of the boys playing were telling an adult about their proton packs. They all decided they should make slime for the packs. We found a recipe and the children decided they needed to add small pieces of coloured paper, which they cut up.

They then carefully filled the proton packs. This activity was great for practising cutting and controlling a spoon to fill the packs. We also spent time talking about our recipe and reflecting on how we could make the slime better.

Creative development:

- Creating our own superhero costumes
- Inventing superhero characters or backgrounds and props for superhero play
- Offering open-ended resources, such as large pieces of material to be capes
- Encouraging loose-parts play for children to construct their own narratives
- Engaging in messy play, for example, making slime
- Using our imaginations when engaging in fantasy and role play
- Inventing logos or recreating standard logos using different media.

Using the environment to allow playful aggression and minimise violence

Some Canadian research found that antisocial behaviour and violent play reduces when there are more manipulable materials available in the environment (Brussoni et al., 2017). Children who are able to move things around, play physically engaging games and invent their own environment are usually more engrossed in their play and more likely to play with a purpose in mind, leaving less time for poor behaviour, boredom and violence.

There are still relatively few research projects that consider the importance of allowing children to engage in more aggressive play, although, in general, it is accepted that all types of play are beneficial to children's development. As Hart and Nagel (2017, p. 45) state: "The intolerance of preschool children's playful aggression may reduce their optimal development; more specifically, young children's cognitive, social, physical and communicative development may be deprived of developing to the fullest extent." As educators, we can use superhero play as a context to include more playful aggression, which will, in turn, allow children to fully develop skills such as resilience, problem solving and social competence.

I was recently invited to support a large inner city school in London that was struggling with the behaviour of its intake of very boisterous boys. I led some training that focused on promoting positive behaviour and we talked about using conflict resolution and emotion coaching strategies to support this group. The educators shared their thoughts about how these children really needed a more physically active environment so we discussed ways in which to make this possible. The two nursery classes were adjacent to one another with a large space between the two rooms. The educators decided to use this as a rough and tumble space, equipping it with soft-play type materials. Children would be allowed to access the space during free play sessions and sometimes specific children would be invited to use this space at other times if they needed to let off steam or be more physically active. I am looking forward to revisiting this school to see the extent to which this rearrangement of the environment has helped with this group of children.

Case study – early years teacher and parent

"Recently my son has shown a lot of interest in guns and other military weaponry, but he didn't seem to be doing much else with them apart from firing bullets and the like around the house. Alongside this, he has a real fascination with his little box of army toy soldiers. He often lines them up meticulously and uses them in imaginary pretend play, much like we observe the children using the small world resources in nursery. By talking with him I discovered he had a lot of interest in the goodies/baddies element of 'teamwork' and fighting the 'bad guys'. He also often asked about the 'war' so this led us to the library for some books.

"As an early years teacher I am used to creating exciting environments as provocations for children to explore and investigate. I decided to create a tuff tray 'desert' as a base for the soldiers. It was lovely to see my three children collaboratively play. They made campfires, discussed 'base camp' and which country they were from. I noticed 'killing' was never mentioned directly but they acted out 'defeat' by knocking over soldiers and burying them in sand. This was not violent play despite it being in the context of war, instead it was playful aggression and tactical warfare. A lot of the play also involved their army 'working together' to build things – they added our Jenga blocks, which I thought was pretty resourceful! I also liked how they discussed which country they were from, lots of links to learning!

"I usually work with babies, so delving into a slightly older age group was really fascinating. I began feeling unsure about encouraging weapon and gun play and questioned if providing an army provocation was really an appropriate thing to do. But on reflection, I think it gives them a safe space to explore different roles and identities, and power and authority."

Sometimes we may identify that a specific child needs additional support and engaging in superhero play and playful aggression may be just the therapy she needs. Bayley and Featherstone share a story about such a child, "Michael the superhero" (2010, p. 71), who had had a difficult start to his young life. They talk about this play as being therapeutic for Michael as he received many benefits from playing at superheroes. They also honestly share about how tricky things were for them, as educators, to embrace his play. Some of the girls were frightened of him and he got up to all sorts of mischief from climbing on the roof to spin a web to running everywhere at the speed of light and wielding various weapons! In spite of all this they state: "There was no doubt about it; superhero play was Michael's salvation. In spite of a sad personal history, he was an extremely lively and happy four year old" (2010, p. 71).

They link the success of his engagement in playfully aggressive superhero games as helping him to feel like he has an element of control in his life. "Superheroes are invincible, they rescue people and have special powers such as the ability to fly or climb high buildings. They can destroy enemies with a wave of the hand or even a look! How attractive this must be to a small vulnerable boy, who feels powerless to control his own life (Bayley and Featherstone, 2010, p. 77). For Michael, engaging in superhero play made all the difference.

In summary

Creating a learning environment that encourages superhero play is easy when we let the children guide our planning. There are some super resources available to support educators in our role; however, perhaps the best resources are the simplest. The "material tied around a child's shoulders" type of cape and the stick that is pretending to be a gun are cheap and easy ideas to implement. These ideas build on children's own resourcefulness and encourage creativity. There are also a large number of story books that we can use in relation to superheroes. These can be useful for generating ideas and sparking interest, however, it is important to allow children time to create their own stories too.

Many settings use Vivian Gussin-Paley's style of storytelling (1984, 2010) or have embraced the idea of *helicopter stories* (Lee, 2016) when children perform their own stories, written down by an educator and re-enacted by the author and their friends on a simple stage marked out on the floor of the classroom. I want to end this chapter sharing about a time when I was lucky enough to sit in on some helicopter stories performed by children aged between three and four years old in Widcombe Acorns Preschool. One story is particularly close to my heart. The author, Lizzie, a fairly new child to the setting, had just turned three, appeared shy and had very little spoken language. She was still settling in to the strange, exciting new world of preschool!

An educator marked out a stage on the floor using masking tape in a little quiet room just off the main play space. A small group of children gathered in anticipation in the space while the educator explained that they were able to make up their own stories today. She asked the children one by one what their story was and quickly wrote it down. She then asked the children if they would like to perform their story on the stage. All of the children were very excited at the prospect of this and eagerly agreed. Amazingly, Lizzie wanted to go first. She only had one character in her story. Lizzie took centre stage and the educator read her story: "Once upon a time a superhero."

Lizzie proudly struck a pose with one arm in the air and the other behind her in a classic Superman flying sort of way. Everyone clapped. This power pose was so poignant for her to make and was moving to watch. Her peers enjoyed seeing her perform and didn't seem to mind or notice that the story ended before it had really begun! Lizzie looked delighted and was even more thrilled when the educator said that she would tell Lizzie's mum about her amazing story.

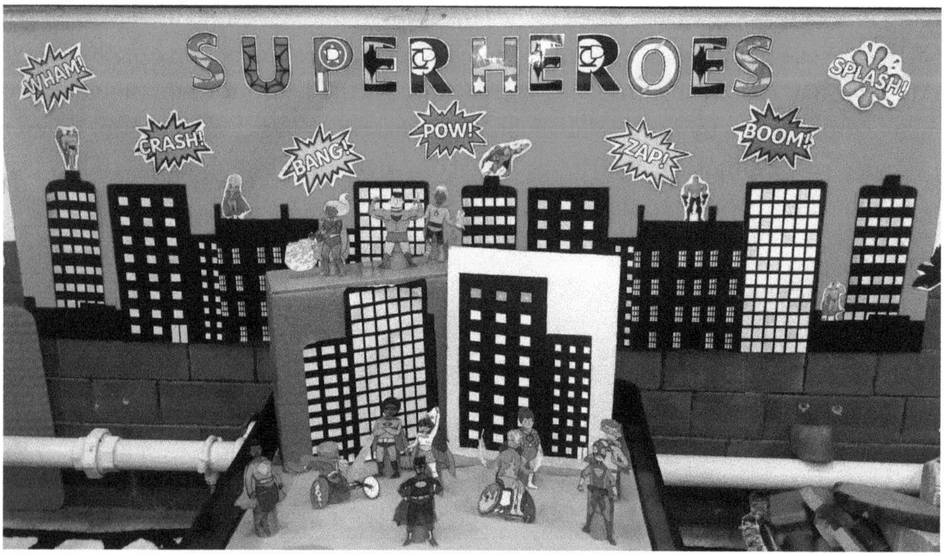

Through offering opportunities for superhero play, we can provide an environment for all children that really is enabling, we just need to listen to them, observe closely and link in with their interests.

Questions for reflection

1 How can you create an enabling environment that embraces superhero play?
2 Can you think of ways to extend and develop children's superhero storylines?
3 What skills will children develop if they create their own props and weapons? How can you resource the environment so that this is possible?

References

Bayley, R. and Featherstone, S. (2010) *The Cleverness of Boys*. London: Featherstone Education Ltd

Brussoni, M., Ishikawa, T., Brunelle, S. and Herrington, S. (2017) Landscapes for play: effects of an intervention to promote nature-based risky play in early childhood centres, *Journal of Environmental Psychology, 54*, pp. 139–150

Department for Education (DfE) (2017) Statutory framework for the early years foundation stage. Retrieved from http://www.foundationyears.org.uk/eyfs-statutory-framework/

Edwards, C., Gandini, L. and Foreman, G. (2012) *The Hundred Languages of Children. The Reggio Emilia Experience in Transformation*, 3rd edn. Santa Barbara, CA: Praeger

Gussin-Paley, V. (1984) *Boys and Girls. Superheroes in the Doll Corner.* Chicago, IL: University of Chicago Press

Gussin-Paley, V. (2010) *The Boy on the Beach. Building Community through Play.* London: University of Chicago Press

Hart, J. L. and Nagel, M. C. (2017) Including playful aggression in early childhood curriculum and pedagogy, *Australasian Journal of Early Childhood, 42*(1), pp. 41–48

Jazwierska, Z. (2003) Spider-Man: practicing mindfulness and increasing focus. Retrieved from http://kidsrelaxation.com/uncategorized/spider-man-practicing-mindfulness-and-increasing-focus/

Lee, T. (2016) *Princesses, Dragons and Helicopter Stories.* London: David Fulton.

Montessori, M. (1936) *The Secret of Childhood*. London: Longman,
Green & Co.

Papatheodorou, T. (2010) The pedagogy of play(ful) learning environments. In Moyles, J. (Ed.) *Thinking about Play*. Maidenhead: Open University Press

Pound, L. (2005) *How Children Learn.* Leamington Spa: Step Forward Publishing Limited

Vygotsky, L. (1978) *Mind in Society: The Development of Higher Psychological Processes*. Boston, MA: Harvard University Press.

Xiong, S. (2017) Equity vs equality vs justice: how are they different? Retrieved from https://www.icafoodshelf.org/blog/2017/11/15/equity-vs-equality-vs-justice-how-are-they-different

8 "Freddy's gonna 'get' you!"

Effectively managing superhero play

Introduction

For many leaders and managers within early childhood settings, superhero play is very difficult to deal with. It might involve balancing the needs and interests of the children with supporting members of staff with very different viewpoints and parents who may support or strongly oppose this type of play. There are advantages and disadvantages when adopting different approaches to managing superhero play and each needs to be considered thoughtfully within your own context. What might work well in a large inner-city setting might not work in a small rural one or an approach adopted by a setting catering for children of military families may not be appropriate for a setting that caters for a different group of children. For some providers, it may appear to be the easy option to limit superhero play or ban gun play outright. However, a simple ban may not be the best option for the children.

Decide on your approach

Many settings opt for a zero-tolerance approach to any play that could potentially involve violence, aggression or play fighting. This usually includes superhero play, as this can be deemed as aggressive and can include rough and tumble or weapon play. A zero-tolerance approach involves an educator shutting down any play episodes that begin to encroach on, or could lead to, this play, steering the children in other directions or directly telling the children that they are not allowed to play out certain themes. The ethos behind such a ban can be based on sound principles, for example, fighting is wrong and hurtful and we do not want to include any games that hurt other people. It could be argued that we should be protecting children from things such as weapons that are designed to hurt, destroy or even kill and, instead, should be teaching them values such as love, peace and how to get along with other people rather than engage in war. Although I understand and sympathise with this viewpoint and totally agree that we should teach loving values, I can also see how a direct ban of this play can have a negative effect, as we discussed in Chapter 2.

As Rich notes when sharing the various reasons that practitioners give for taking a zero-tolerance approach: "The list [of reasons] is practically endless, although the comments usually end with, 'But they do it anyway'" (2003, p. 2). This is not to say that it is a fait accompli and therefore, because weapon play is inevitable, we should allow it for that reason alone, as I do not feel that this is a strong argument. However, it should be noted that when we try to prevent children from playing games that come naturally to them, they will find ways around this and we may be inadvertently encouraging children to be deceitful.

Case study – zero-tolerance approach

Four-year-old Ben spends a long time building in the construction area. He is creating something that looks suspiciously like a gun. Mrs A approaches Ben and asks him what he is doing: "I'm making something miss. It's not a gun …" "That looks interesting, what is it if it's not a gun?" "Umm … it's, it's a zapper miss!" "A zapper, and what does a zapper do?"

Ben looks sheepish, then triumphant and says: "A zapper changes the TV channel ..."

When out of earshot of the adults Ben was observed zapping children and "killing" them, when within earshot he was changing their channels!

Many educators can relate to a version of Ben's story above, when a child knows that he is creating something he shouldn't and so he makes up a story to cover up this fact. Ben knows it's a gun. Mrs A knows it's a gun. A "zapper" even points at things and zaps like a gun. But Ben, at his tender age of four, knows that if he wants to continue with his game he needs to lie and cover up the real game he is playing. Mrs A will turn a blind eye to this game if he says it's a zapper and he can continue to make his gun in peace.

This is not OK! Ben is in a class where children have a huge range of interests from dinosaurs to fairies and from Star Wars to Cinderella. We should celebrate these interests and our love and care for children should not be conditional. Ben feels that he has to lie to be accepted, yet his friends can play openly engaging in themes relating to their interests. What has he done to deserve this? Nothing! We should not be creating an ethos where children feel that their interests are wrong, bad or unacceptable. Surely we should be giving children the message that they are welcome here, they are accepted unconditionally and we appreciate who they are, interests, fascinations and all.

Therefore, banning superhero play can, in practice, sometimes lead to children becoming deceitful and, as a forbidden fruit, can actually make the play more appealing to others! In Ben's setting, the hard-line no-gun policy had encouraged him to deceive the adults in the setting and cover up his true intentions. Not really a skillset we would want to encourage!

Case study – discussing an alternative approach

One setting discussed whether or not to follow a zero-tolerance approach after one cohort was particularly engrossed with superhero play and, unfortunately, this led to several incidences when children got unintentionally hurt. Parents complained and the manager felt under huge pressure to ban this play from continuing. Thankfully, the setting had a play policy in place which talked about allowing children the freedom to play and follow their interests without being limited by adults. This enabled the manager to put measures in place to supervise the play more thoroughly while still allowing the play to continue and gave her confidence when talking to the parents about this decision.

So as a leader or manager in a setting, we are faced with a choice: do we ban this play to try to avoid children being hurt, limit ramifications from parents or as a moral stance? Alternatively, we could actively encourage this play and see it as an opportunity to work within children's interests and teach the children skills and attitudes that will support them further in life. Is this a black and white choice? I think not. There are settings that have successfully allowed children to engage in superhero play where they do not get hurt any more than usual and parents are happy with the levels of supervision in the setting. In addition, there are settings that have gone the whole hog and actively encouraged children to pursue these interests where, again, this play is managed appropriately, parents appeased and accidents limited. It doesn't have to be an all-or-nothing choice, but I believe a zero-tolerance approach should be avoided if possible.

Instead, it is important to engage in a professional dialogue about superhero play in its widest context and explore everyone's thoughts and feelings about it. There needs to be a non-judgemental atmosphere so that all members of the team feel able to talk openly. It is vital that if there is any disagreement about what our approach should be, all contrasting views are discussed in terms of advantages and disadvantages and not simply dismissed. Any changes made to practice should happen at a rate where everyone feels comfortable. I have found a useful rule of thumb when reflecting on practice to be considering the benefits (or otherwise) to the children. The Bristol Standard Quality Improvement Framework "enables settings to continually reflect on their practice to improve the quality and effectiveness of their provision for all children and families" (2018) and encourages providers to consider their strengths, what they want to improve and how this will benefit the children. If we follow this pattern, we keep children at the heart of our discussions and can consider the best approach to suit them.

Put a policy in place

The setting above was able to stand firm in what they believed because they had a policy in place underpinning their practice. Policies outline our actions and procedures and should underpin our practice. They ensure that everyone involved with the setting understands what we do in practice, when and how we do it and why we do things this way. Policies enable us to be transparent about the ways in which we safeguard, care for and educate the children. Our policies also help us to be consistent in our practice and are a great way to share this with parents and carers. When new parents engage with our settings, we should ask them to read our policies and procedures and sign to show that they have done this.

There is no requirement to have a policy relating to superhero play, however, I have found that if you put your ideas in writing this makes your ethos clear and transparent to everyone. Ideally, all policies are discussed as a whole team and written to reflect your practice and ethos, then shared with parents and carers and children in an age-appropriate way. This is about deciding what you believe is right for young children and stating it for everyone to see.

Your setting is unique, therefore it is vital that you talk about your own premises, circumstances, practitioners' beliefs and discuss the children you care for, their background and experiences and ensure that your policy reflects this. It needs to take into account the various viewpoints represented in the setting and consider how comfortable staff feel about superhero play in practice. One way to do this is to think in terms of "when a child … adults will …" For example, when a child engages in rough and tumble play, adults will supervise to ensure that all children are happy or when a child makes a gun, adults will talk to them about their design. In addition, in the same way that we have considered children's perspective and any benefits to the children when deciding on our approach to superhero play, we must ensure that we consider the voice of the child when writing our policy.

A superhero policy could include the following points:

- How you have observed children play in your setting.
- Your rationale about superhero play – what you believe and why.
- Your approach – how you will respond to superhero play, e.g. role model, join in, supervise.
- An acknowledgement that there are different perspectives on this.
- How children have been involved or their voice is represented in the policy.
- How you will liaise with parents and carers.
- When you will review the policy and evaluate how things are working.

An example of a policy can be found in Appendix 1 and can be adapted to meet the specific needs of your setting.

Once the policy content is discussed and agreed by the team, it can be written up and shared with parents and carers and implemented. You will want to ensure that all stakeholders have a copy and are aware of this and all your policies.

Design appropriate rules

When putting policy into practice, it is sensible to consider the rules and boundaries you might have in place to keep children safe and review these in the light of superhero play. Some settings include superhero rules as part of their usual rules, other settings feel that their general rules apply and are enough as they wouldn't want to burden children with more rules to keep! Anni McTavish talks about creating a superhero code of conduct: "To help children take responsibility for deciding their own, positive rules for energetic play" (2009, p. 13). Children regularly talk through their storylines and the rules before they begin to play so whenever possible, allow them to create their own rules, role modelling or offering scenarios if needed.

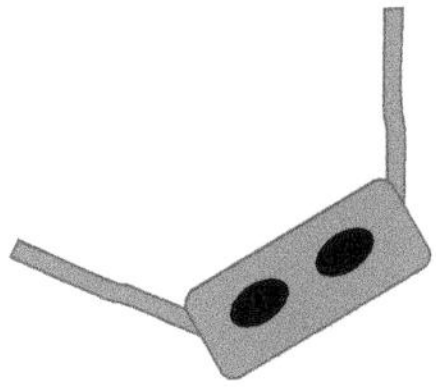

Our superhero rules

Superheroes...

1. ...rescue and protect other people
2. ...do not hurt others
3. ...only shoot people who are part of the game

The sorts of rule you might want to consider should include boundaries about personal space and hurting others, for example, superheroes have kind hands and feet or superheroes help, not hurt, others. Also rules relating to engaging others in the play, for example, superheroes invite others to play or we only shoot other people who are in the game. This can help to avoid the scenario when children are trying to engage others in the game who don't want to play. As discussed in Chapter 2, it can also be useful to agree a pause button or way to stop the play with immediate effect. This could be calling "Freeze!" or having a specific word which everyone agrees will cease play, for example, "Stop!" Helping children to be in control of when full body play starts and stops is also an important way to empower children and safeguard them. If children know that they can say "Stop it, I don't like it!" at any time and that other people MUST stop at that point, they might feel more confident if they need to safeguard themselves in the future.

When deciding on your rules, you may not feel that you can go into the detail that Jane Katch (2001, p. 92) went into with her group of almost bloodthirsty children when they set their rules:

1 No excessive blood.

2 No chopping off body parts.

3 No guts or other things that belong inside the body can come out.

Jane shares that her children regularly engaged in what she calls "violent play" and felt that they needed specific rules to support them. They were using graphic and violent language in their play and replicating this in their rules helped to ensure compliance! In addition to these rules, children were only allowed to play these games in alternate "recesses" or playtimes, to ensure that children who didn't want to play in this way could still play with those who did want to play these games.

Once we have established our rules, we need to advertise them and make sure that everyone is aware of them. So make a poster or banner displaying the boundaries that have been set. Anni McTavish (2009) suggests that a mini-version of this poster could be shared with parents and carers to involve them in this process and ensure that they are aware of the boundaries agreed. Children can be rewarded and praised for keeping the rules or for demonstrating that they can play in a "super" way.

Superhero Licence

Superheroes help other people
Understand and keep rules
Persevere and keep trying
Everyday we try to do our best
Respect and care for others

Building on this idea, another setting decided that they would license children to become superheroes and in doing so the children had to conform to a set of rules. This setting used a generic set of rules for all children, but we could consider personalising the rules on the licence if it was deemed appropriate to do so. This idea links nicely with encouraging children to adopt superpowers of their own and the sorts of powers they might be, for example, resilience and perseverance. Chapter 10 thinks about this in more detail.

Do your research

Superhero play needs to be discussed as a team so that everyone responds consistently and in line with our ethos and policy. It can be really helpful to know a little about the characters that your children are most interested in, so do some research to find out about the various superheroes. Find out their names, then learn what their superpowers are and perhaps memorise a few key phrases that might be typical for them to say, for example: "To the Batmobile" (Batman or Robin) or "It's time to be a hero!" (PJ Masks). Appendices 2 and 3 include charts that I hope you will find useful. They outline the various superheroes and offer a little context. You may occasionally come across a child who has an encyclopedic knowledge about superheroes; this can be very useful as you can ask them questions, however, it can also be tricky when they "correct" you and other children!

There are also supervillains that we need to know about because each set of stories usually introduces an enemy or nemesis for our heroes. It is worth knowing the names of some of these, too. Some children might want to play a character of a supervillain and they may or may not know that they are a baddie, therefore we could find that we need to support a child who wants to play a supervillain as a goodie. If there is a more knowledgeable superhero fan (child) in the setting, she might insist that she is a baddie, so it can be handy to prepare for this and have a scenario up your sleeve, for example, pretend that the Joker had a magic potion that turned him good ...

Knowing the backstory or a little context about the various superheroes can be really useful even if the children do not appear to know this detail themselves. Taking a keen interest in the various superheroes demonstrates that we are interested in things that they like. This validates children's feelings, values their interests and makes them feel special. We can also use this context to help us intervene more sensitively or become a co-player more successfully. Many times I have tried to engage in superhero play with children and felt out of my depth as the children know the special powers and abilities of the heroes much better than I. We can also ask children to tell us about their heroes. In this scenario, children become the more knowledgeable other and often enjoy teaching us all that they know, enjoying the fact that they know more about this than their educator. The educator at Widcombe Acorns understood that the children wanted to impress her with their knowledge and she gave them space to do this in without interrupting, then she began to sing the Spider-Man song and the boys were thrilled.

Case study – Widcombe Acorns

Josh and Jack were dressed as Spider-Man in the role play area. They were discussing what they were going to do. Josh said: "We're going to be bad Spider-Man, so let's pretend to be good Spider-Man, but really we're going to steal things!"

Both boys laughed and ran off.

Later on these boys were talking to an adult: "Superheroes have superpowers. Superman, Spider-Man and Batman. Super Josh and Super Jack!"

They were keen to "teach" the adult everything they knew about the various superheroes and were amazed when she responded by singing: "Spider-Man, Spider-Mman, does whatever a spider can ...!" The boys joined in: "catches thieves just like flies ... Watch out, here comes Spider-Man!" They laughed and then struck the iconic Spider-Man pose, with two fingers and thumb strategically placed in the "I'm about to cast out a web" sort of way. They both ran off again, still in role talking again about baddies. The interest of these boys and their friends in superheroes led to the setting putting on a hero-themed play which the children performed for the parents, choosing the Spider-Man theme music to dance and move to.

In addition, knowing about the backstory and context of a superhero also offers us opportunities to talk about tricky subjects like death, dysfunctional families or celebrating diversity because the majority of superheroes have a story to tell. We can identify with Peter Parker (aka Spider-Man) who lives with his loving aunt (and uncle) or sympathise with Bruce Wayne (aka Batman) who was sadly orphaned when an attempted burglary went wrong. Alternatively, we can talk about similarities and differences and discuss the X-Men who were born with specific powers and abilities (mutants).

Other ways that you can manage this play is to:

- Allow children time and space in which to engage in superhero play; this will help to prevent it from spilling into times (if any) when you would prefer them to refrain from this play.
- Support the children as they set the scene by talking through the characters and storyline.
- Help them to make any props that might be useful.
- Talk about who the goodies and baddies are and what they do.
- Extend the narrative if children get stuck at "bish, bash, bosh!"
- Problem solve when difficulties arise.
- Use conflict resolution and emotion coaching techniques to resolve any conflicts.
- Find out about the moral principles that many superheroes stand for and include them in the game.
- Try not to take over their play and storylines – it's their play and you should be sensitive to this.
- Equip your book corner with stories of heroes and use these themes as opportunities to engage children in reading and writing as well as imaginary play.
- Give children choices and power in real life as well as within the games, for example, present children with options about what to play with next or what to eat from a menu of healthy snacks.
- Keep an eye on the time so that the children can find a resolution in their game before the next transition, e.g. tidy-up time or lunch time.

One setting created props with the children to help enhance their superhero play. They painted boxes and stuck "windows" on to create skyscrapers and also invested in some small world characters in addition to creating some child-sized superheroes.

Linking with home

Sometimes children's play is a window into their lives and we can gain a picture of what is happening at home by observing them. Safeguarding children remains at the heart of what we do in our care for young children and we must ensure that if their play gives rise to any concerns about the child we must act on it.

Case study

After Halloween, Damon was talking in detail about Freddy Krueger the character from *Nightmare on Elm Street* and telling children that if they weren't careful Freddy would "get them". The manager of the setting approached his parents to talk about this as she was concerned that Damon had been watching an inappropriate film. In discussion with his parents, they discovered that Damon's teenage brother had been babysitting at the weekend and Damon had been channel hopping and watched part of the film. They had strong words with the teenage brother and talked to Damon about the character, that he was not real and would not "get you" or "get" anyone else.

In the above case study, the educators felt compelled to intervene and find out more about what had happened at home regarding the programme that Damon had watched. This was a difficult conversation for the educator to have with the parent and sometimes, in order to successfully manage tricky situations, we need to have difficult conversations. My colleague Annie Davy calls these "courageous conversations". Here are some steps which will help you to handle these discussions in a positive way:

Step 1. Remind yourself what is motivating you to have the conversation, for example: "We need to explore what is going on for Damon because he needs to keep bringing scary stuff into his play."

Step 2. Find the right time and place to have the conversation and ask permission to talk about the situation.

Step 3. Start with see/hear language that is non-judgemental and keep the child central to the discussion, e.g. "We have noticed that Damon has been wanting to incorporate scary themes into his play ..."

Step 4. Find out what the other person knows about the situation and try to ascertain how they feel about it. Avoid making generalisations or assumptions.

Step 5. Be specific and direct and check that you are being understood and be as empathetic as possible where you are putting yourself in their shoes. This is different from being sympathetic, which can come across more negatively as showing pity or feeling sorry for them.

Step 6. Offer a way forward or solution if appropriate and allow the other person to ask questions.

As educators we often hear a child say words and phrases or act in ways that are surprising, endearing or are a little grown-up in style, then we meet their parent and everything makes sense! This should not be surprising, because we know that a key way children learn is through imitation. We need to ensure that we are working in partnership with parents and carers with regard to superhero play, just as we do with regard to all other aspects of practice. Chapter 9 looks into this in more detail.

Try not to micro-manage this play!

I love the title of one of Julie Fisher's books, *Interacting or Interfering?* (Fisher, 2016). It says it all, doesn't it? There are times when I know I have unintentionally interfered rather than interacted. We need to allow our children the freedom to engage in play themes without taking over or limiting their narratives. Children rarely have opportunities to play freely away from the prying eyes and ears of grown-ups and Gray suggests that we should be concerned about the way that children's play has been increasingly taken over by adults (Gray, 2013). If we continue to do this we deny children the opportunities to resolve conflicts, problem solve and learn about social interaction for themselves.

We do, however, sometimes need to directly teach children strategies to use to enable them to become more independent in their own social interactions and superhero play offers us an ideal opportunity for this. It may involve us role modelling, demonstrating strategies, directly and indirectly teaching children what to do and how to do it.

An excellent example, which offers us a step-by-step guide of how to do this, is the HighScope problem-solving approach to conflict resolution (2018). It changes a fight, argument or disagreement into a problem that needs to be solved and is outlined in Table 8.1. Ove time, through adopting an approach such as this, children will learn to resolve their own conflicts and disputes for themselves. You may even find that the first time you realise that there has been a problem is when the children ask you for a sandtimer or to help you with their solution!

Table 8.1 Problem-solving approaches

The problem-solving approach to conflict resolution	Example of using this approach in a setting Isaiah and Alex were fighting over the Batman cape. The argument was escalating and the boys were about to start physically hitting one another. Sarah, an early childhood educator, stepped in.
Step 1. Approach calmly, stopping any hurtful actions or language	"Hey Isaiah and Alex, what's going on? Remember to use kind hands ..." She stepped between the two boys and gently held the cape, allowing them both to keep holding it, too.
Step 2. Acknowledge feelings	"Alex, you look very angry and Isaiah, you look very cross too!"
Step 3. Gather information	"What happened?" The boys both tell Sarah about the cape and how they both (!) had it first. The tug of war starts again. Sarah holds the cape still. "Let's hold the cape together."
Step 4. Restate the problem	"Now, it looks like we have a problem guys because we only have this one Batman cape and (counts) one, two, children want to play with it."
Step 5. Ask for ideas for solutions and choose one together	"What shall we do?" Several children have now begun to watch this interaction. Sarah asks them for ideas, too. One child suggests that they buy a new cape but Sarah explains that although a good idea, that won't solve the problem right now. Then Isaiah says: "I know! Maybe Batman and Superman are fighting, so we could get a Superman cape too?" Alex thinks that this is a good idea but still wants the Batman cape. They agree to play Batman versus Superman.
Step 6. Give follow-up support as needed Adapted from HighScope Educational Research Foundation (2018)	Sarah helps Isaiah to find the Superman cape and put it on. She then checks that Alex is happy with the arrangement. She says: "Well done guys, you really are superheroes! You solved the problem!"

In summary

Superhero play can present managers of settings a various number of challenges, but it also presents them with numerous opportunities. It is our role as educators to use these opportunities for the benefit of the children. To do this justice, we need to decide as a team what our approach to superhero play is then adopt this as policy and set rules accordingly. We also need to do our research and find out about the popular culture characters that our children are most interested in and use this information to support and extend children's play, working in partnership with parents and carers. Lastly, we must ensure that we do not interfere too much with their play and then managing superhero play to minutiae becomes superfluous!

Questions for reflection

1 In what ways do you find managing superhero play challenging or otherwise?
2 Could you conduct a risk/benefit analysis of superhero play to weigh up the advantages and challenges?
3 Is this type of play covered by any of your current policies? If not, what could you include in a superhero policy?
4 Are there opportunities to notice children keeping your rules and being gentle and kind when engaging in superhero play?

References

Bristol Standard leaflet (2018) Retrieved from https://www.bristolearlyyears.org.uk/wp-content/uploads/2018/07/BD10722-The-Bristol-Standard-WEB-2018.pdf

Fisher, J. (2016) *Interacting or Interfering? Improving Interactions in the Early Years*. Maidenhead: Open University Press

Gray, P. (2013) *Free to Learn: Why Unleashing the Instinct to Play will Make our Children Happier, More Self-reliant, and Better Students for Life*. New York: Basic Books.

HighScope Educational Research Foundation (2018) How does High/Scope help children learn how to resolve conflicts? Retrieved from https://highscope.org/faq

Katch, J. (2001) The rule of violence, *Independent School*, 60(4), pp. 92–94

McTavish, A. (2009) 50 *Exciting Ideas for Using Superheroes and Popular Culture* Cambridge: Lawrence Educational

Rich, D. (2003) Bang, bang! Gun play, and why children need it. *Early Education Journal*, 2003. Retrieved from http://dianerich.co.uk/pdf/bang%20bang% 20gun%20play%20and%20 why%20children%20need%20it.pdf

9 "He practically lives in his Spider-Man costume at home ..."

Engaging with parents about superhero play

Introduction

At home, pop culture is prevalent as children watch films and cartoons, play technological games and collect merchandise and toys relating to their viewing habits. Superheroes play a large part within this culture. Children wear superhero pyjamas and other superhero clothing, then there are specific dressing up-costumes and small-world play, technological games, not to mention TV programmes and movies that relate to superheroes. Many children have superhero parties and the majority of children's cartoon series will come with their own range of merchandise aimed at getting the child hooked on the product ... For example, at the time that *Frozen* was released there were very few households in the UK that managed to stay thawed – that is, *Frozen* free! We saw this first hand with the CBeebies character Tree Fu Tom. Our youngest daughter loved watching the programme and her birthday list included Tree Fu Tom shield and gloves as well as character mini-figures.

Thus, superhero play in all its many guises is a very common type of play for children to engage in at home. While settings may have firm rules and boundaries in place about superhero play, for example, rough and tumble play or playing with guns, the home environment is often very different with sometimes contrasting rules and boundaries. This is appropriate as home needs to be a place in which children can unwind, relax and be themselves.

Many parents and grandparents will engage in rough and tumble games with their children and grandchildren and this is perhaps one of the earmarks of the intimate relationship that families have. My children will regularly jump on me or have a tickling match; likewise we have different types of guns and weapons to enhance their play in the house and garden.

Parents and practitioners can understand why it is appropriate for home and setting to have a different set of rules and boundaries, however, it can be really difficult for children to understand these differences. We are often striving for consistency between home and setting in relation to behavioural expectations, thus why should it be any different for superhero play? For the purposes of this chapter, I am using the term parents to include a child's main carers as well as biological parents.

Case study

Scenario 1: visiting a friend's house The children use the guns and bows and arrows to engage in a make-believe game of chase and shooting. The adults loosely supervise as they catch up on any news over a cuppa, only really getting involved when a child comes for help. Meanwhile the children run inside and out, happily shouting and calling to each other.

Scenario 2: in the playground
The same children continue their game of chase, albeit without the added weapons. The adults tell them to be careful and chastise them when they get too noisy. As soon as it appears like someone has been hurt, the game is banned. The disappointed children are wondering what the difference is between their games that are acceptable and those that are not.

Scenario 3: in the setting
The children are running inside and out, chasing each other. One child wears a cape and builds a gun out of stickle bricks, then pretends to shoot the others. A practitioner joins the game, she soon gets shot and the children need to call a doctor to help her. A child runs inside and grabs the doctor's case, rushing to help the injured practitioner. The practitioner recovers quickly, helped by the medical assistance and asks another child to help her make a gun out of the Lego so that she can retaliate ... The game continues for a sustained period involving all parties until tidy-up time.

In the first scenario – at the friend's house – these games were accepted and pretty much ignored by the adults. This is often the situation in the home, when parents sometimes expect the children to entertain themselves. They are not too worried what the game entails so long as the children are happy and play nicely together. In the second scenario, the game was banned before the children had the opportunity to develop their play further.

In the third scenario, the practitioner embraced the play by playing along and also encouraged more elements of role play, asking for medical assistance. She engaged more children in the play by asking for help to build a gun with the Lego. Surely this should be our role as an educator; playing alongside children, being a role model and finding ways to extend children's play when it is appropriate to do so.

Research

We are all aware of the expression "Parents are a child's first educator"', but when a child starts in a setting, his education at home does not stop there. Parenting, for all its joys and challenges, is a continual process of education and growth, for both the parents and the children! There is a wealth of research that reiterates the importance of parents being interested and involved in their child's education, thus part of our role is to engage and involve parents in our settings (Desforges and Abouchaar, 2003). Harris and Goodall (2008, p. 287) state: "Without doubt, parental engagement in children's learning makes a difference and remains one of the most powerful school improvement levers that we have." They propose that educators need to ensure that parents know the powerful influence that they have and that this will involve a concerted effort and commitment of time for both parents and educators. Their research is in line with the findings of the Effective Provision of Pre-school, Primary and Secondary Education (EPPSE) study, which found that *what* parents did to encourage their children to learn was more important than who they were in terms of economic status or educational level (Baker et al., 2014; Mayo and Siraj, 2015).

The Early Years Foundation Stage Statutory Framework in the UK acknowledges the partnership between parents and educators stating that: 'Good parenting and high quality early learning together provide the foundation children need to make the most of their abilities and talents as they grow up" (Department for Education (DfE), 2017, p. 5). There is also a wealth of research demonstrating the importance of early intervention and the difference that this can make to children and their families. The Foundation Years report *Preventing Poor Children Becoming Poor Adults* (Field, 2010, p. 6) acknowledges that: "Nothing can be achieved without working with parents" and so fully engaging families and intervening early can help ensure that children reach their full potential.

It might be helpful to think about our work with parents by using the model proposed by Degotardi and Pearson (2014), which considers parents, educators and child as three sides in a triangle of care, all equally important and all contributing to the relationship. In addition, they note that all of these relationships are interrelated and each will impact on the other. In the past the main caregiver with whom educators engaged was usually the mother, but as parenting has changed over the years, generally speaking, fathers have taken on much more of an active role, which means that, as educators, we often interact with both parents and sometimes grandparents and other carers, too (McHale, 2007). Therefore when we think about engaging with parents we must do so in its broadest sense and include extended family members and other carers as appropriate. This model is also helpful in the way that it includes the child in this relationship – we should always ensure that children remain at the heart of any discussions between educators and parents.

Involvement or engagement?

We regularly talk about getting parents involved in our settings but some theorists distinguish between involvement and engagement and suggest that engagement is a better way to think about this topic. Rather than thinking about getting parents *involved with the setting* we should think about getting parents *engaged with children's learning* (Goodall and Montgomery, 2014). This brings the focus of attention for both the parents and setting firmly onto children's learning. This is a shift in emphasis which avoids the "them and us" mindset, but instead implies a partnership working towards the shared goal of supporting the child in their learning. It also keeps the child central to everyone's thinking.

Case study – childminder setting

One childminder worked closely with parents and encouraged them to focus on their child's learning by inviting parents to share what they were learning at home. She used the term "proud clouds" and sent home templates that parents could choose to complete if they wanted to. These were then displayed on her noticeboard for a few weeks then contributed to the children's learning journey books.

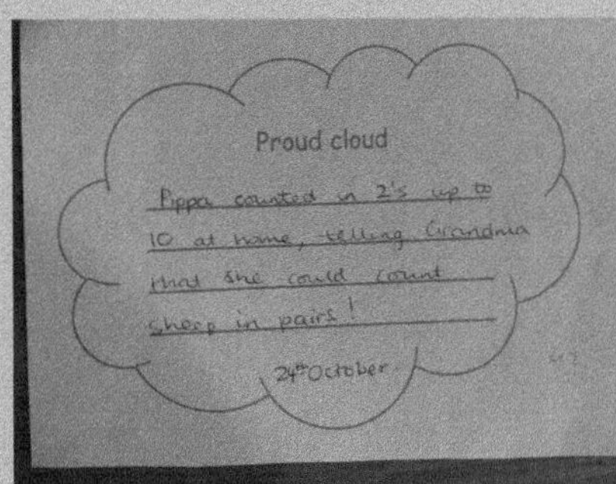

The report "Provider influence on the early home learning environment (EHLE)" was commissioned by the then government in order to "help identify what nurseries and other early years settings could do to better support parents to develop their children's learning at home" (DfE, 2010, p. 6). Building on research suggesting that parental involvement and engagement is vitally important for educational achievement, the report offered practical advice for educators about successful strategies that they could use when engaging parents. Their research used the Early Home Learning Environment Index to identify opportunities taken by parents that support home learning. There are seven activities included in this index:

1 Parent reading to the child

2 Parent taking their child to the library

3 Child playing with letters
4 Parent helping their child to learn the alphabet
5 Parent teaching their child numbers or counting
6 Parent teaching their child songs, poems or nursery rhymes
7 Child painting or drawing at home.

These activities do not require any specialist equipment and could be as simple as a parent counting the steps as they walk upstairs or pointing to a letter on a road sign that is the same as the initial letter in their child's name. During their research the amount of home learning that parents engaged in with their children was measured before a child started in a funded childcare setting and again six months later. They found that after six months of attending a childcare establishment, parents increased the range of home-learning activities that they undertook with their children as a direct response to support they received from educators.

The report noted that the most successful engagement methods for parental engagement were:

- Face-to-face and one-to-one interaction
- Having an open-door policy
- Communicating during drop-off and pick-up times
- Offering "stay and play" sessions for parents to attend with their children
- Inviting parents to workshops, meetings and events
- Providing information about opportunities for learning at home
- Home visits, when educators visit children in their homes
- Sharing information about their child and their progress. e.g. Early Years Foundation Stage Profiles or learning journeys.

The research found that around two-thirds of parents attended events at their childcare setting aimed at collaborative working between home and setting and of these a staggering 97% of parents tried home-learning activities suggested to them at these events (DfE, 2010, p.16), demonstrating face-to-face events as being one of the most effective ways to encourage parents to engage in home learning. The report also found that one-third of early years practitioners felt they needed to increase their confidence levels when working with parents and wanted more help and information on how to engage parents in early home learning. Leaders and managers of settings have a responsibility to ensure that their staff feel equipped and confident to engage parents and carers effectively.

Barriers to engagement

Parents will engage with our settings with varying levels of involvement and this is determined by a number of factors that we may need to address or barriers that we need to overcome. Here is a list of potential reasons why parents may find it hard to get involved:

- *Time.* Many parents work full or part time and may not have much time to be commit to the setting.
- *Attitudes.* Perhaps parents feel unwelcome or uncomfortable with engaging, this may be their first encounter with "education" since being at school themselves and their prior experience may not have been positive.
- *Confidence.* Many parents are unsure of the contribution they can make and might not feel confident to engage with the setting.
- *Jargon.* Within education as a whole, it is very easy to fall into using technical language and jargon and this can make it harder for parents to engage with us.
- *Bias.* Perhaps we have our own biases about which parents will and won't engage with us and this can become a self-fulfilling prophecy.
- *Language.* Many parents' home language may not be English and often the parent who is in charge of childcare is less confident in English than the parent who may, perhaps, be using English more frequently at work.
- *Stigma.* Some parents may feel uncomfortable about getting involved with the setting because they do not want to appear needy or are perhaps embarrassed about the level of support that they receive.
- *Culture.* There may be cultural differences that make parental involvement more difficult, for example, Iranian families will avoid making eye contact as a sign of respect and humility, which is at odds to British culture, which expects eye contact to be made.

You may have come up with many more barriers and there will also be some that are very specific to you in your unique context. It is important to consider which barriers are pertinent to you and how you can overcome them in order to successfully engage parents.

Hornby and Lafaele (2011) have come up with a model of factors that act as barriers to parental engagement and involvement as shown in Table 9.1 below. They propose that educators can use this model to help them to explain, interpret and address issues relating to parental engagement.

Table 9.1 Factors that can act as barriers to engagement

Individual parent and family factors	*Child factors*
■ parents' beliefs about parental involvement ■ perceptions of invitations for parental involvement ■ current life contexts ■ class, ethnicity and gender	■ age ■ learning difficulties and disabilities ■ gifts and talents ■ behavioural problems
Parent–teacher factors	***Societal factors***
■ differing goals and agendas ■ differing attitudes ■ differing language used	■ historical and demographic ■ political ■ economic

(**Source:** Hornby and Lafaele, 2011, p. 39)

There have been numerous studies that consider how the various barriers can impact levels of involvement and engagement and I am unable to consider each barrier in detail in this chapter. Some barriers appear to be harder to overcome than others, for example, how we encourage parents from different cultural backgrounds and those who are linguistically diverse to engage with our settings. These families need greater advocacy than other families (Öztürk, 2013) and educators may need to specifically target this group to find ways of reaching them, arranging activities and offering a welcoming, inclusive ethos that values diversity and allows families to feel comfortable whatever their background.

A super resource I have come across that helps to bridge the language barrier with families is the PenPal or Talking Pen. Developed by Mantra Lingua (2019), the UK-based

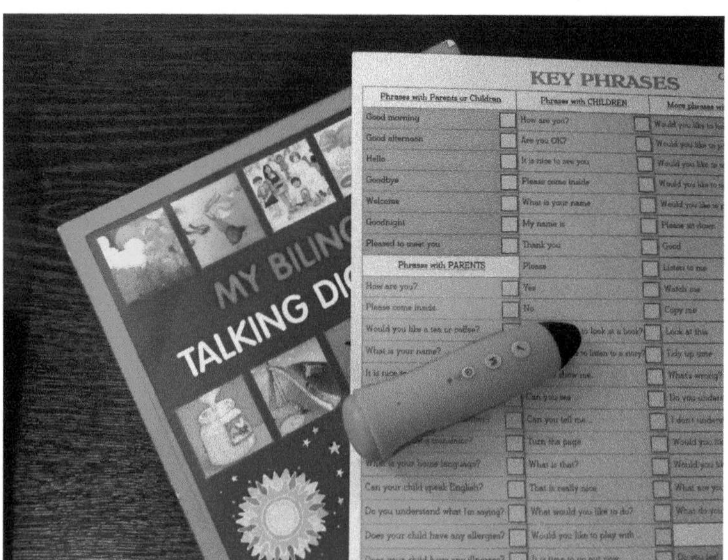

publisher specialising in multilingual resources, the pen can "read" the text in whichever language it is programmed to use. The pen "reads" a series of little dots in the same way that a barcode scanner scans a barcode. The pen can store data like a USB storage device does and you simply ensure that the languages you need are stored on the pen. You can purchase a key phrases chart, which includes the various phrases you might need in a basic meeting with parents and the pen is compatible with hundreds of dual-language books. If you have any dual-language books in your setting, you will probably find that they are published by Mantra Lingua (2019) and can be read by PenPal.

It is also helpful to consider representation of different groups of parents in our settings, for example, fathers, parents who live apart from their children and working parents. We can use superhero play as a fun way to build up relationships with parents by sharing ideas of superhero activities they can try at home. Encourage parents to watch superhero programmes with their children like *PJ Masks*, *Tree Fu Tom* or *Go Jetters* and talk about the ways that the characters are being heroic, e.g. rescuing people or helping someone who is afraid. Share simple ideas for resourcing this play like providing some material to be a cape or making a mask together.

Case study – out and about!

The great thing about superhero play is that children and families can engage in it at any time without needing expensive resources or equipment. While my friend was on a family picnic, a blanket became a superhero cape and her daughter skipped around saying: "Look at me, I'm flying and I'm going to save the world again!"

I have read many reports, articles and books about parental engagement and many of these refer to "hard-to–reach" parents. These are parents who are on the fringe of our setting or who come from backgrounds that research shows are less likely to get involved with settings and attend events. However, the term "hard to reach" is very one sided, suggesting that it is the setting that is doing the reaching out and finding it difficult. Although this is sometimes the case, it could be argued that many parents feel that settings themselves are hard to engage with (Day, 2013). In addition, Crozier and Davies (2007) suggest, stating that some parents are just harder to reach can also be useful, excusing us from being more proactive in our attempt to engage parents. It might be helpful, therefore, to reframe this phrase, flip it and consider from a parent's perspective whether our own setting is somewhat "hard to reach".

When engaging with families, it is vital that we are able to see the perspective of parents because this will allow us to understand their family and empathise with the many pressures that they are under. In order to do this, we must try to ascertain their views and build strong relationships with parents. We start developing these relationships from the outset, as soon as parents first consider using our setting. It is worth noting that transitions can be difficult times for children and parents alike. Many families struggle when their child first goes into an early childhood setting. Sometimes engaging in play that is very familiar to the child and family can really support them during this transition. Superhero play can bridge this gap as many children arrive in our settings already interested in heroes and parents are familiar with these icons. We can use these themes to help children to settle in quickly and help parents to feel at ease. Degotardi and Pearson (2014) emphasise the importance of establishing shared expectations and priorities between parents and educators and superhero play offers an ideal opportunity within which to teach the rules and boundaries that keep everyone safe.

Case study – ensuring an open dialogue with parents

In one setting, a parent complained because her son, Henry, was engaging in gun play. She felt it was inappropriate for a nursery to allow this sort of play. Thankfully, the setting had a clear policy that this parent had read and signed when the child started at the nursery so the manager was able to stand firm on this and explain their ethos for allowing gun play. The manager encouraged the parent to share exactly what it was that she was worried about and then tried to resolve the issue. It turned out that the mother had banned guns because they hurt people and Henry had become obsessed with guns, turning anything and everything into a gun. The manager explained that they understood her viewpoint but wondered if banning gun play was making it even more attractive to Henry and gently suggested that she reconsider and see what happened over time. The mother decided to compromise and allow guns if Henry made them, for example out of a stick or Lego. After a month, the manager revisited this conversation with Henry's mum and she revealed that Henry's obsession had, indeed, lessened – perhaps as a result of gun play no longer being forbidden.

The relationships that we build with parents should be authentic and reciprocal in nature, allowing communication to flow in both directions. When we demonstrate to parents that we want to hear their ideas and opinions and that they have skills and abilities that we would love them to share with us, we also prove that we value them and respect their viewpoint.

The views of the child

Another very successful way of engaging parents is to keep their child at the heart of what we do. When we consciously put children first we also want to ensure that we take into account their views so that their voice is heard when it comes to any decisions relating to them. Listening to young children is a recurring theme within the early years sector with many settings adopting the "mosaic approach", which considers the views of young children and attempts to respond and actively listen to their perspective (Clark and Moss, 2011). Considering children's views in a holistic way will help to keep the child at the heart of early years practice.

It can be difficult to take the views of young children into consideration because they may not yet have the language skills needed to articulate their ideas and thoughts, however, it is still possible to ascertain their views. For example, we can observe children closely, watch where and how they play, notice their preferences in terms of play mates and what they interact with. Even babies can communicate their feelings when we remain sensitive and actively tune into them.

Listening to children is vitally important – we can find out all sorts of things about our children. For example, when my friend was talking to her three-and-a-half-year-old daughter about what she wanted to be when she grew up, the child's response was really endearing and surprising! She said: "Um, well. I love you mummy ... but when I grow up I'd like to slay a dragon!" As educators we use what we know about the children to personalise their learning experience and parents know their children better than anyone, so asking parents their perspective on their children's views can be an eye opener and really useful.

Engaging parents and children using superhero play

Superhero play provides an accessible context within which to engage parents with their children's learning. You could provide ideas of how to support children at home through play and talk to parents about what they have noticed that their children can do at home and share what they do in the setting. You might like to create a "story sack" around superhero play for children to take home which could contain a book, jigsaw, mini-figures and opportunities for mark making. Including a note to parents which explains the benefits of superhero play may also be a useful way of engaging parents with children's learning.

Case study – superhero family fun

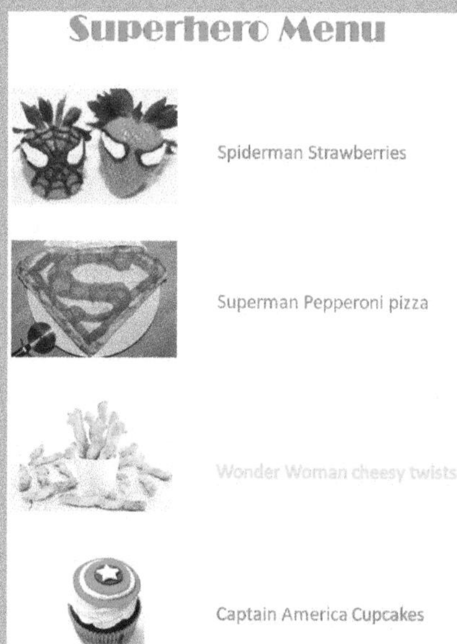

Superhero Menu
Spiderman Strawberries
Superman Pepperoni pizza
Wonder Woman cheesy twists
Captain America Cupcakes

One setting invited children and parents/carers to return to preschool from 4pm until 6pm for a superhero family night. They invited children (and adults!) to dress up as their favourite character and attend the setting to engage in fun activities. During the day the children had created superhero snacks to share with their parents at this event. Then during the evening they made superhero masks, played superhero logo bingo and had various family challenges to complete, such as crawling under Mission Impossible-style woollen webs without touching the wool. The educators also shared with families what children are learning through superhero play and the various rules and boundaries that they set. A "super" time was had by all!

Many therapists use superheroes to support them in their work with children as superheroes provide a great context for talking through many issues. Role playing different scenarios might help a child to manage her feelings and behaviour (Rubin and Livesay, 2006). We can encourage parents to also use this theme if it supports them in their role of helping their child. For example, I created this scale at home based on various versions available commercially for my daughter with an interest in superheroes. It helps us to talk together about how angry she feels and what she can do about it.

5	I am out of control and feel like I am going to explode. I want to scream and hit. I need to calm down.	
4	I am getting very angry and am starting to lose it! I need to get away fast.	
3	I feel a little out of control or over excited. I want to run away as fast as I can! I need to do something calmer.	
2	I feel a little worried or frustrated. I will try to get through this! I need to be careful not to get overwhelmed.	
1	I feel good! I'm completely in control! I'm happy!	

Engaging with parents is not about treating all children and families the same, but being equitable with them. The children we look after are all unique and their family lives will be diverse so we need to adjust our ethos and teaching in the light of this. For some children, we may need to consider specific interventions to support them and plan these in conjunction with parents. The nursery below also used superhero play, in the guise of Gladiator fights, to help Oliver who was struggling with anger issues. They had to work closely with his parents to work towards resolving this tricky situation.

Case study – supporting an angry child in partnership with parents

In our nursery we had a four-year-old boy, Oliver, whose parents were separated. On certain days of the week he stayed with his mum and on others he stayed with his dad. We began to notice a pattern that on the days that he had spent the night at his dad's house Oliver would arrive at nursery really angry, tearing in, red in the face, fists clenched and shouting and roaring at everyone. Immediately he would proceed to throw items around the room, for example, trains from the trainset or the kettle from the home corner. He was not deliberately aiming these at anybody, but if another child were in the way, he occasionally got hurt.

We also noticed that on the days where he was due to go to his dad's that night he would start to get very angry and wound up towards the end of the session. He would be calmly playing with playdough for example, then would start to squeeze it tightly, rip it aggressively into little shreds and throw it on the floor, while going red in the face and starting to growl and roar. By story time he would be unable to sit down or focus on anything and would be running and shouting round the room pushing chairs over and hitting children and adults.

We felt we needed to address this behaviour and had regular meetings with his parents and with various outside professionals who came into our setting to observe him and advise us. To help him calm down and manage his anger, we would take him and two other boys out into the garden where they could engage in "Gladiators-style" superhero battles. They would all have a long foam poles, around six feet long, and they were allowed to batter one another with these poles for 10 or 15 minutes. The other boys laughed at such a fun game, but for Oliver, it really helped him to externalise his anger in a safe way. He knew the "rules" for this game, for example, if one of the others said "Stop", he had to stop etc. Once we could see that a lot of the aggression had gone, Oliver would come back inside and go into his safe place (a tent in the corner) until he felt ready to come out. We often knew when he felt better because he would invite a friend into this tent with him for a few minutes before they would emerge together and continue with the game they had started in the tent.

We also talked to Oliver about managing his anger and how it wasn't acceptable to throw toys. When he was calm he was the loveliest, politest little boy who completely understood, but when he was angry it was like he was lost in this terrible rage. We worked closely with both of his parents and documented everything. He successfully moved on to school quite soon after these episodes where we hope he has settled in well.

Practical ideas about how to engage parents in their children's learning:

- Discuss superhero play with parents and carers and try to ascertain their views.
- Ask for help from parents with anything from gardening or sharing a hobby to being an extra pair on hands on a trip or leading a cooking activity with the children.
- Value all contributions that parents make.
- Parents generally love to talk about their children so ask for information about the children's interests and abilities.

- Ensure all information sent home is accessible to parents and carers of all backgrounds (use plain English and think about providing text in different formats/languages/large print etc.)
- Find out about the parents of children in your setting – use their gifts and talents or consider using their professions to widen the children's experiences.
- Invite families to attend a short superhero workshop for parents and children to learn together.
- Share some superhero activities that parents can try at home with their children.

In summary

Superhero play offers educators numerous opportunities to link with families as this play considerably overlaps with things they will engage in at home. The examples at the start of this chapter also highlight the additional freedom that many children experience when playing at home. They may have greater access to specific toys like weapons and have more opportunities to engage in unsupervised play. In addition, at home, rough and tumble play comes into its own with many parents engaging in very physical games with their children.

Many parents see the benefit of these games at home as contributing to close relationships and being fun for all involved. We need to think about involving parents in terms of engaging them with their child's learning and address any barriers that may get in the way of this. By building effective relationships with parents and keeping children at the heart of our practice, we can help our little superheroes to flourish both with us and at home.

Questions for reflection

1 To what extent are parents engaged with their child's learning at your setting?
2 Are there any ways in which your setting is hard to reach?
3 How do you empower parents to feel valued and understand the influence that they have on their children's learning and development?

References

Baker, W., Sammons, P., Siraj-Blatchford, I., Sylva, K., Melhuish, E. & Taggart, B. (2014) Aspirations, education and inequality in England: insights from the Effective Provision of Pre-school, Primary and Secondary Education Project, *Oxford Review of Education*, *40*(5), pp. 525–542

Clark, A. and Moss, P. (2011) *Listening to Young Children: the Mosaic Approach*, 2nd edn. London: NCB

Crozier, G. and Davies, J. (2007) Hard to reach parents or hard to reach schools? A discussion of home–school relations, with particular reference to Bangladeshi and Pakistani parents, *British Educational Research Journal*, *33*(3), o. 295

Day, S. (2013) "Terms of engagement" not "hard to reach parents." *Educational Psychology in Practice*, *29*(1), pp. 36–53

Degotardi, S. and Pearson, E. (2014) *The Relationship World of Infants and Toddlers* Maidenhead: Open University Press

Department for Education (DfE) (2010) Provider influence on the early home learning environment (EHLE). Retrieved from https://assets.publishing.service.gov.uk/ government/uploads/system/ uploads/attachment_data/file/181753/DFE-RR142.pdf

Department for Education (DfE) (2017) Statutory framework for the early years foundation stage. Retrieved from https://www.foundationyears.org.uk/files/2017/03/eyfs_ statutory_framework_2017.pdf

Desforges, C. and Abouchaar, A. (2003) *The Impact of Parental Involvement, Parental Support and Family Education on Pupil Achievement and Adjustment: A Literature Review*. London: DfES

Field, F. (2010) The foundation years – preventing poor children becoming poor adults. Retrieved from https://webarchive.nationalarchives.gov.uk/ 20110120090141/; http://povertyreview.independent.gov.uk/media/20254/poverty-report.pdf

Goodall, J. and Montgomery, C. (2014) Parental involvement to parental engagement: a continuum, *Educational Review*, *66*(4), pp. 399–410

Harris, A. and Goodall, J. (2008) Do parents know they matter? Engaging all parents in learning, *Educational Research*, *50*(3), pp. 277–289

Hornby, G. and Lafaele, R. (2011) Barriers to parental involvement in education: an explanatory model, *Educational Review*, *63*(1), pp. 37–52

Mantra Lingua (2019) Retrieved from http://uk.mantralingua.com/

Mayo, A. and Siraj, I. (2015) Parenting practices and children's academic success in low-SES families, *Oxford Review of Education*, *41*(1), pp. 47–63

McHale, J. (2007) When infants grow up in multiperson relationship systems, *Infant Mental Health Journal*, *28*, pp. 370–392

Öztürk, M. (2013) Barriers to parental involvement for diverse families in early childhood education, *Journal of Educational and Social Research*, *3*(7), pp. 13–16

Rubin, L. and Livesay, H. (2006) *International Journal of Play Therapy*, *15*(1), pp. 117–133

10 "To infinity and beyond!"

Encouraging children to find their superpowers!

Introduction

The CBeebies website has a quiz inviting children to answer a variety of questions and find out which superpower would suit them. Children love this sort of thing and we could easily create our own quiz. Identifying that a superpower such as flying, incredible strength or super speed would suit a certain child is a bit of fun. However, we can also talk to the children about real superpowers, powers that make a difference in our everyday lives. For example, kindness, patience, perseverance, resilience and having a "can-do" attitude. Many of these powers can be identified within the Characteristics of Effective Learning (Department for Education (DfE), 2017), which are the dispositions that early childhood educators try to instil in our young children.

I believe that all children are competent learners and have within them the necessary skills and abilities to become heroes and potentially change the world! There is something really powerful when sharing with children about other children and young people who have done something truly heroic or are making the world a better place in some small way, for example, Greta Thunberg, the Swedish teenager who has challenged the world to combat climate change. There is a great website called Kids are Heroes (2019) dedicated to sharing such stories. Their stated mission is "to empower children from all cultures to become social change agents" and they particularly focus on humanitarian issues relating to changing social habits and values in order to positively impact the environment, animals or other people.

When considering how we can all make a difference in the world, I am reminded that my youngest daughter loves the starfish meme adapted from a story by Eiseley (1978) and often asks me to recount it before bedtime. It goes something like this: One day a man was walking along the beach when he noticed a little boy picking something up and throwing it into the sea. On approaching he realised that the beach was covered in tiny starfish and the young boy was throwing them back one by one. He asked the lad what he was doing and was told: "The tide is out and these starfish will die if I don't throw them back into the water." The man smiled at his naivety and gently said: "But there are so many, you can't possibly make a difference!" The little boy didn't answer immediately, he simply picked up another starfish and threw it into the ocean, then he said: "It made a difference for that one!" Such stories can really inspire young children and can act as a conversation starter about how even small acts of kindness can make a huge difference.

Chapter 6 explored how we can use real-life heroes to explore heroism and this chapter takes this a step further by considering how we, too, can be heroes. Remind the children that: "With great power comes great responsibility ..." and that it is important to use our strengths for the benefit of others.

The importance of body language

Early years educators understand the importance of body language with young children because language development begins with a stage of preverbal communication. This involves very young children using gestures and noises to make their intents known to others. Once children master talking, they rely on gestures less, however, we all continue to use nonverbal communication throughout our lives. The main ways that people communicate with each other are listed below:

- Sounds (uh, mmm, brrr etc.)
- Crying, gurgling, babbling, squealing
- Gestures
- Pointing

- Body language
- Eye contact/ eye movement
- Sign language – if known
- Speech (words, intonation, volume).

There are various studies that claim that the majority of our communication is nonverbal and Argyle, Alkema and Gilmour (1971) found that of the two channels of communication humans use, verbal and nonverbal, it is the latter that holds more weight and so there is some truth in the expression that "actions speak louder than words!"

With this in mind, I was interested to read some research that suggests that adopting a power pose or superhero stance positively benefits your state of mind. Equally, I have read some research that contradicts this and suggests that adopting a power pose does not have any impact on behavioural outcomes. Despite these conflicting viewpoints, it is fair to say that our body language affects our outlook. For example, if we feel happy we tend to smile, however, if we force ourselves to smile, even if we don't feel very happy, we will begin to feel happier! (Kar and Kar, 2017). We can teach children to have good posture, smile and therefore develop children's self-esteem. Chapter 7 ended with a story

about Lizzie who adopted her own power pose when she told her story. The pose gave her confidence and I'm sure that the positive response of the educators will also have helped to build her self-esteem.

Superhero backstories and context

The major superheroes features in films and cartoons have myths and backstories that attempt to explain where their superpower has come from. It can be useful to be aware of these and Appendix 2 is a guide to knowing your superheroes. There are a mix of characters who have a dark secret past like Batman and others who gain their superpowers from more alien sources and are strongly linked with truth and light, like Superman. Others become heroes by accident or through scientific experiments like Spider-Man and the Hulk, while others are simply born that way, like the X-Men (Rubin and Livesay, 2006). Many of them have suffering or a tragic upbringing as a common thread, which had led them on the righteous path of trying to save the world or make it a better place.

When appropriate we can share these backstories as a context for our own little heroes, explaining how these people overcame opposition or loss and have made the decision that these experiences will not negatively impact their future. Instead, they have learned from past mistakes or trauma and grown stronger as a result. We can link these ideas with stories of people in real life who, it could be said, have shown superhuman strength and overcome oppression or adversity. These figures could be historical greats like Rosa Parks or contemporary heroes like Edward Whipple, an American boy, who created a 3-D printed arm for a little English girl.

Empowering the adults who work with your children

In order to instil superhero qualities in our children, we need to empower the educators who are working with them and ensure that they feel looked after and equipped to fulfil their roles. If we are stressed or feel unhappy at work, this will rub off onto the children and they will pick up on these feelings. The Talking About Wellbeing project, a joint venture between the National Children's Bureau and colleagues from Early Childhood Studies at London Metropolitan University, identified that staff need to have high levels of resilience and wellbeing in order to have a positive effect on children's wellbeing (Manning-Morton, 2014). In her recent book, my colleague Sonia reiterates this as she notes the most important way that educators can promote children's emotional health and wellbeing is to have good wellbeing themselves (Mainstone-Cotton, 2017). She suggests educators should be kind to themselves, consider their working environment and engage in effective supervision where everyone can be open about their feelings and honest about their emotions.

Case study – Winsor Primary School

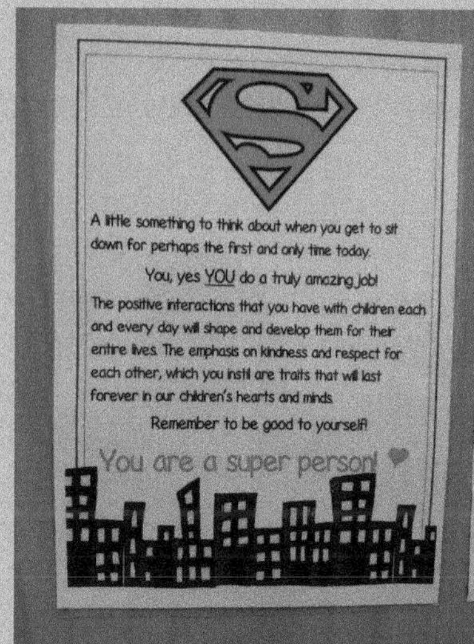

A little something to think about when you get to sit down for perhaps the first and only time today.
You, yes YOU do a truly amazing job!
The positive interactions that you have with children each and every day will shape and develop them for their entire lives. The emphasis on kindness and respect for each other, which you instil are traits that will last forever in our children's hearts and minds.
Remember to be good to yourself!
You are a super person!

While on a recent visit to Winsor Primary, I was thrilled to see this great poster on display on the back of the staff toilet door! The poster (originally sourced from a tweet) encourages staff in their role and reminds them to look after themselves, as this forms the basis for their relationships with the children. Their school vision is to create an environment that is purposeful, inclusive and engaging at the heart of their culturally rich and diverse community. They want children to grow into resourceful, independent learners and develop a thirst for learning that will stay with them throughout their lives. It strives to do this with a team of dedicated and extraordinary educators and staff wellbeing is seen as vitally important.

Looking after your own wellbeing can be as simple as talking about your feelings, keeping active and eating and drinking healthily. Sometimes we may need to ask others for help or take a break and we need to acknowledge that these are signs of strengths and not weaknesses. In order to explain to children that even superheroes need to recharge their powers sometimes, we must be actively role modelling how to rest, calm down and look after ourselves. You could role model this by trying the Spider-Man meditation in Chapter 7 with your children.

Helping children to become responsible citizens

Several years ago, it was popular to discuss citizenship in schools and how to encourage children to become good citizens. Through the Every Child Matters agenda, this idea morphed into how we support children to be healthy, stay safe, enjoy and achieve, make a positive contribution and achieve economic wellbeing (DCSF, 2008). Now there is a large emphasis on supporting children's wellbeing and mental health, although it has yet to make it into a statutory document. However, throughout all of these different political and fashionable agendas, one thing has always remained true – that adults who work with children want the best for them and want them to achieve their potential and grow up into the responsible adults. This is not simply about empowering children to have a growth mindset or to instil the dispositions and attitudes that they need in order to be successful in life, it is wider than that. It involves other people, living as part of a community and impressing on children, from an early age, that we are responsible for our actions and how they affect other people.

Case study – charity cake sale

When our oldest daughter was four years old she read about the low numbers of Rockhopper penguins and decided to organise a charity cake sale in aid of them. She invited our neighbours and her preschool friends to come and buy a cake and she donated the money to the RSPB to go towards helping these vulnerable creatures.

In addition to making and decorating the cakes and with only a little help from me, she created posters explaining about the Rockhopper penguins and why we should help them. The event was a great success and is an example of how we can all be heroes in our own way.

It could be argued that we live in a "rights" generation when children are growing up aware of their rights and knowing what expectations of them are realistic. This is not implicitly wrong; I could cite plenty of situations when this attitude has safeguarded children or helped to remove them from potentially abusive situations. However, in this "me-first, others last" scenario, children are not always taught how their actions and decisions can affect other people.

I have sometimes heard of modern children being referred to as the "snowflake" generation. Each child grows up knowing that she is special and unique, which are beliefs that I would want every child to have, but not at the expense of others. We are all important, as important and special as everyone else, but not more important or more special than everyone else, because holding this belief puts other people down. So children must learn that what we do and say will affect others positively or negatively. We live in a community with others and children must learn about give and take in relationships.

Another great way to teach children about responsibility is to encourage them to care for an animal. Many schools and settings have pets, which are a useful way of encouraging children to look after others. Although rather a morbid thought, as discussed in Chapter 3, they can also be a way of introducing children to the concept of death as many pets have a short lifecycle and children may experience them dying while they attend the setting.

In addition to caring for a pet there are other ways that we can encourage children to become responsible. For example:

- Caring for other people, i.e. younger children in the setting
- Recycling items helps us to care for our world
- Giving away some toys to a charity shop
- Being kind to others just because we can be
- Visiting a nursing home or residential home
- Hatching frogspawn or butterfly eggs
- Organising a charity event that the children can get involved in, i.e. Toddle Waddle for the charity Meningitis Now
- Sharing stories about people who need to be responsible for others
- Fostering a volunteering mindset.

Case study – Odstock Nursery

Every year as part of core planning, all ages look at lifecycles and each age group has the opportunity to care for chicks or froglets or butterflies. One of our principles underlying this work is not to steal the learning. For example, if we always give children the answers, we have stolen the opportunity for them to learn. So when some eggs are delivered with an incubator to our children, we deliberately do not tell them what we are hatching. From this provocation, the children begin to investigate where eggs come from and speculate about what could have laid these eggs and what creature will hatch out of them. They might find out that snakes and butterflies lay eggs, but so do duck-billed platypuses and dinosaurs. Through conversations, books, pictures and stories we can explore these ideas and offer children time to discover for themselves. This gives children a real sense of awe and wonder as well as great excitement!

Encouraging our children to be super-friends

One of the key ways that we can use superhero play is to enable children to develop friendships and understand the qualities it takes to be a good friend. I have come across a fantastic idea of how to broach this topic with very young children; it is called bucket filling and is the brainchild of McCloud (2013). The story shares that everyone carries a bucket – they can fill other people's buckets through acts of kindness or empty other people's buckets by being unkind or not doing the kind thing they could do. Every time we interact with others, we have the option of figuratively filling or emptying their bucket. In my view, real-life heroes are bucket fillers, people who think about others and are considerate about how their actions will impact on them.

This links in with young children's understanding of theory of mind, as mentioned in Chapters 5 and 6. Children find it difficult to empathise and truly understand the implications and consequences of their actions. We can support children to develop this understanding by:

- Being consistent in our responses to children.
- Setting rules and boundaries and explaining them to children in age-appropriate ways.
- Talking about feelings and emotions regularly as part of our daily practice.
- Role modelling and explicitly talking through how our actions will affect other people.
- Share stories with children that look at choices and relationships, such as *Have You Filled a Bucket Today?* (McCloud, 2013)

Harris shares stories about how the role of the superhero has taken on a positive twist in her preschool classroom as children demonstrate sensitivity towards a child with disabilities, shy children grew in confidence in the playground and a child with an overpowering older sibling learned how to feel masterful and powerful in his own right (2016).

Empowering children to develop friendships and understand how to become a good friend is perhaps one the greatest gifts that we can bestow on the children in our care.

An additional theme we can harvest is that of teamwork. Several superheroes work in a team and collaboration with their friends is vital to their success in the mission, for example, the Fantastic Four, Go Jetters or PJ Masks. Children generally begin to play collaboratively from around two and a half years old. Prior to this, children are mainly playing alongside others, watching them or playing alone. We can help children to learn to play collaboratively by explicitly talking to them about friendships and reading them stories that focus on friendship like *The Rainbow Fish* (Pfister, 2007) or *This is Our House* (Rosen, 2007). In addition, we can plan activities specifically designed with team playing in mind. Parachute games are a fun way of encouraging very young children to work together and to realise that their actions might impact on someone or something else.

Children sometimes have misconceptions or funny ideas about friendship, so when talking about how to be a super-friend with young children discuss different ideas about friendship. Can we be friends with more than one person at once? Is it OK if I like different things from my friends? Celebrate the similarities and differences between one another and acknowledge that being a good friend does not mean you cannot play with anyone else.

There are also different activities we can do to promote friendship and being a good friend. We can use stories, puppets, props, role play, photos of our friends and scenarios about good (and bad?) friends. These are the sorts of idea that you might want to instil. Super-friends:

- Are loving and caring
- Know that a smile can make a difference to someone's day
- Have kind hands and kind feet
- Notice if a friend looks sad
- Sometimes play games that their friends choose and sometimes play games that they choose
- Are polite to one another
- Listen to what their friends say
- Invite others to join in.

Superpowers for super kids!

We all think our children are amazing, but they really are! They just don't always know it! We can instil in them the sorts of superpower that will help them to develop into well-rounded adults. We need to talk to children about their own superpowers and how we can develop them. Ideas of superpowers that you may want to encourage could include:

- Kindness
- Looking after others
- Being loving
- Forgiveness
- Having self-control
- Peacemaking
- Goodness
- Precision
- Friendliness
- Listening
- Self-regulation (managing big feelings)
- Gentleness
- Memory
- Fairness
- Hopefulness
- Persistence
- Joyfulness
- Curiosity
- Growth mindset
- Being a bucket filler (as discussed earlier in this chapter).

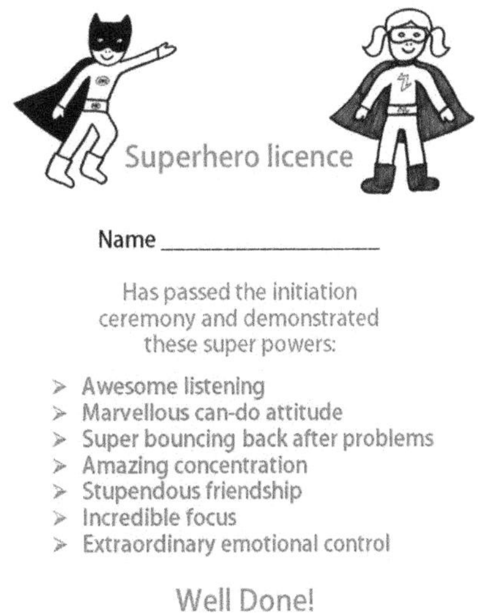

Superhero licence
Name ________________
Has passed the initiation ceremony and demonstrated these super powers:
➢ Awesome listening
➢ Marvellous can-do attitude
➢ Super bouncing back after problems
➢ Amazing concentration
➢ Stupendous friendship
➢ Incredible focus
➢ Extraordinary emotional control
Well Done!

These and other such "superpowers" should be valued and fostered through our ethos, policies and practice and it is also helpful to share with the children the sorts of qualities that we consider to be superhero powers. One setting decided to create superhero licences to celebrate the development of these attributes and parents were invited to a special initiation ceremony when the children were presented with these licences. Other ideas are to play "spot the superpower" and celebrate such attributes when they are observed in our friends or create a kindness jar or kindness diary to store the acts of kindness that have been shown.

Case study – kindness jar

The idea of a kindness jar is that the children help to decorate a very special jar and you keep some pieces of paper and pens nearby. When someone witnesses someone else being very kind, they write it down, fold the paper and put it in the jar. Then every term or every few months you can get the notes out of the jar and read them, celebrating the many acts of kindness that have taken place.

We can be heroes!

As discussed in Chapter 6, talk to your children about what a hero is and discuss the qualities that a hero needs to have. Older children can think about who their heroes are and why those people are their heroes. For example, we can talk to children about ordinary people who do extraordinary things. Within the Early Years Foundation Stage we refer to the characteristics of effective learning (COEL) when we think about what makes a good learner (DfE, 2017). In my opinion, these characteristics also refer to the sorts of skill that a hero needs. For example, a "can-do" attitude and the ability to bounce back after difficulties.

Table 10.1 Characteristics of effective learning

COEL	***Links to heroic actions, beliefs and attributes***
Playing and exploring	Engagement, exploration, can-do attitude, independence, curiosity, fantasy, role play, initiative, risk taking, confidence, adventurousness, courage, audacity, bravery, doing something new, self-belief
Active learning	Motivation, perseverance, persistence, focus, empathy, concentration, asking for help, pride in what they achieve, intrinsic motivation, bouncing back after difficulties, determination, self-regulation and self-control, applying effort, positive attitude
Creating and thinking critically (Adapted from DfE, 2017, p. 10)	Thinking, problem solving, finding new ways of doing things, decision making, prediction, boldness, strength to carry out plans, adapting tasks, changing strategy, planning, not being afraid to change tack if needed, pattern recognition, reviewing tasks

Often themes within superhero play are centred around power and control and, occasionally, this means that it can lead to confrontation and conflict. Although we can use these situations and turn them into opportunities to problem solve and resolve conflict, we also have the option of shaping the play in the direction of teaching children resilience and to gain confidence (Harris, 2016). In one reception class, the children created their own superhero identities, designed costumes and thought of names for their alter egos and, with a little help, had a go at making the costumes. They drew themselves as superheroes and talked about the sorts of superpower they might have. The practitioners skilfully wove together ideas of superpowers such as invisibility and flying with super-listening and resilience. They were able to link this with the characteristics of effective learning and think about concepts such as goodies, baddies, being kind, helping others and obeying rules.

Case study – reception class superheroes

In one reception class, the children were given superhero mini-me characters who were linked to their system of house points. Children could fill the cape with stars for effort or for demonstrating superhero qualities such as resilience and perseverance. This really inspired the children and demonstrated that what the school valued as the praise was not linked to academic achievement but instead was connected to personal superhero qualities.

Here are some of the skills that superhero play can encourage:

- Being a ninja – tiptoeing, quiet movement, sound discrimination, ears are primed to hear the slightest sound.
- Zapping monsters – mastering fears, working out themes relating to good and bad.
- War games – fine motor control, imagination, pretence, self-control, strategy and planning.
- Rough and tumble – bonding, power and dominance.
- Building a gun/weapon – gross and fine motor skills, creativity, imagination.
- Being a spy – writing secret messages, cracking codes, problem solving and completing puzzles.
- Rescuing a fellow superhero – heroism, loyalty, relationships, helping others.

Prerequisites for heroism!

Being a hero doesn't happen overnight! In order for children to believe in themselves, they need to have been loved and cared for. They need to have their basic needs met and feel safe and secure. Within early years, we think about this in terms of having a secure attachment with their main caregiver. Children need support from us as the adults who care for them and they need to feel competent and confident to achieve whatever they want to in life. This will grow from being believed in and told that they are strong and capable. As I write this, I am reminded of an anecdote that one of my students shared with me from her teaching practice. This was in a junior classroom and the student had been given the task of trying to engage a disengaged pupil. She tried to motivate the pupil with no luck, and exasperated, the student went back to the teacher to ask for help. The class teacher sat beside the child, talked softly to him and slowly wrote on a piece on paper in front of the boy. She then got up and moved away from the boy and to the student's amazement, the boy started to write in his book and engage with the lesson. Intrigued, the student walked behind the boy to see what was written on the note to this child. The teacher had written: "You are capable, you are interesting, you are creative." This teacher knew her class well. She knew that this boy hadn't engaged because of his low self-esteem. His teacher demonstrated that she believed in him and he positively responded to this encouragement. We need to instil this belief in our children – that they are capable, interesting and creative and can achieve.

In summary

Superhero play encapsulates engaging storylines and themes that we can use to instil positive dispositions and attitudes in our children. It can offer children opportunities to feel powerful in their heavily controlled lives, simply taking on the posture and stance of a hero can increase levels of confidence and allow children a feeling of mastery. As Harris states: "When guided appropriately in an early childhood classroom, superhero play gives young children opportunities to gain a sense of mastery and empowerment as well as developmentally appropriate benefits by improving language skills, problem-solving and cooperation with peers. By recognising and modelling the characteristics of resiliency and promoting kindness with peers during superhero play, teachers can encourage children to be kind and resilient heroes to classroom friends" (2016, p. 202).

With a little background knowledge, we can use the context of superheroes to set the scene for discussions around families, teamwork and friendship. However, in order to empower children to become heroes, we first need to instil in them confidence and self-belief. We can do this through ensuring that our children feel valued, loved and cared for. In addition, educators need to know their individual children really well and act as a role model when playing alongside them or joining in their games. We can take a leaf from Spider-Man's book and understand that power and responsibility go hand in hand. We have the power, we need to use it responsibly to encourage our children to find their superpowers. So go and fetch your cape!

Questions for reflection

1 How can you instil dispositions such as the characteristics of effective learning in your children?
2 In what ways can you encourage children to become everyday heroes themselves?
3 What superpowers do you value in your children and to what extent do you celebrate them?

References

Argyle, M., Alkema, F. and Gilmour, R. (1971) The communication of friendly and hostile attitudes by verbal and non-verbal signals, *European Journal of Social Psychology*, *1*(3), p. 385

DCSF (2008) Every Child Matters Green Paper. Retrieved from https://webarchive.nationalarchives.gov.uk/20100406190825/http://www.dcsf.gov.uk/everychildmatters/about/aims/outcomes/outcomescyp/

Department for Education (DfE) (2017) Statutory framework for the early years foundation stage. Retrieved from http://www.foundationyears.org.uk/eyfs-statutory-framework/

Eiseley, L. (1978) *The Star Thrower.* New York: Times Books (Random House)

Harris, K. (2016) Heroes of resiliency and reciprocity: teachers' supporting role for reconceptualizing superhero play in early childhood settings, *Pastoral Care in Education, 34*(4), pp. 202–217

Kar, A. K. and Kar, A. K. (2017) How to walk your talk: effective use of body language for business professionals, *IUP Journal of Soft Skills, 11(*1), pp. 16–28

Kids are Heroes (2019) Retrieved from http://www.kidsareheroes.org

Mainstone-Cotton, S. (2017) *Promoting Young Children's Emotional Health and Wellbeing.* London: Jessica Kingsley Publishers

Manning-Morton, J. (2014) *Exploring Wellbeing in the Early Years.* Milton Keynes: Open University Press

Meningitis Now (2019) Toddle Waddle. Retrieved from https://www.meningitisnow.org/support-us/events/fundraising-events/events-by-location/toddle-waddle/

McCloud, C. (2013) *Have You Filled a Bucket Today?* New York: Nelson Publishing

Pfister, M. (2007) *The Rainbow Fish.* New York: North South Books

Rosen, M. (2007) *This is Our House.* London: Walker Books

Rubin, L. and Livesay, H. (2006) *International Journal of Play Therapy, 15*(1), pp. 117–133

11 Concluding remarks

Superhero play in its broadest sense is very popular and can be observed in most early years settings in many guises. We may observe children engaging in fantasy play, taking on the role of a specific character, or roughhousing with their friends. They could be creating weapons from construction materials or recreating a small-world scene with a toy fire engine where firefighters are rescuing people from a burning building. As educators, we have an opportunity to engage with this play, accept it as play and use it to extend a narrative or develop children's own superpowers.

Superheroes are likely to be among us within children's play for a long time to come and should not be viewed as a problem. As early childhood educators, we strive to follow the children's interests and fascinations to create learning opportunities within which children will happily engage and learn, therefore we need to take account of their interests, which regularly lie within popular culture. What they watch, read, play with, the toys in the shops, in magazines and comics and on adverts will naturally feed into their play. They cannot avoid images and characters relating to superheroes and neither should they want to. Children have an urge to play, fantasy and magical thinking still forms a large part of their world and this is a natural part of early childhood.

Part of our role as early childhood educators is to facilitate play by observing what our children do, how they use resources and the themes that regularly lead their play. Then we provide opportunities to extend this play and develop their understanding. It is vital that we accept differences between children's preferences and value their interests, whatever they happen to be. We can use these interests to tailor an exciting and relevant learning environment for our children.

This book argues that a child's interest in superheroes in all its various guises is no less as important and should be equally as valued as an interest in dinosaurs, tractors or princesses. To deny children the opportunity to engage in their interests disempowers them and gives them a negative message about themselves. In contrast to this, educators can use these themes to empower children to learn strategies to resolve conflict and problem solve that will equip them to develop into well rounded adults. Parsons and Howe (2006, p. 298) state that: "Providing opportunities to engage in superhero play opens up a multitude of creative possibilities and allows children the freedom to explore their world

with a sense of empowerment and control." In addition, they can introduce difficult topics, such as war, killing and death, good and evil. According to Kinard, superhero play "is a deep philosophical, psychological, sociological, anthropological exploration of life" (2014, p. 22) and Holland argues that this type of play should be viewed alongside all other types of imaginative play (2003) and not be ostracised or regarded as negative play.

Superhero play can also be a doorway into talking about heroism and the attributes and qualities that we want to foster in our lives. We can share with children stories about real-life heroes and encourage them to undertake their own heroic acts albeit on a smaller scale (see Chapter 6). No superhero book would be complete without a few song references, so we can inspire children to search for their inner hero and become heroes themselves. Encourage them to be good friends and demonstrate superpowers such as resilience and courage. This will enable our children to grow up into the responsible citizens of tomorrow.

References

Holland, P. (2003) *We Don't Play with Guns Here. War, Weapon and Superhero Play in the Early Years*. Maidenhead: Open University Press

Kinard, T. (2014) Flying over the school: superhero play – friend or foe? *Young Children*, *2*(3), pp. 16–23

Parsons, A. and Howe, N. (2006) Superhero toys and boys' physically active and imaginative play, *Journal of Research in Childhood Education*, *20*, pp. 802–806

Appendix 1: Example of a superhero and weapon play policy

At [name of setting] we want to ensure that your children's interests are valued, supported and extended, and we aim to do this through play.

We have noticed that sometimes children engage in play that is influenced by popular culture, for example, playing games related to films, books and TV programmes. Recurring themes regularly include superheroes and weapons. Superhero play encompasses many of Bob Hughes' 16 play types, in particular fantasy play, imaginative play, rough and tumble play and role play. These and other play types are part of normal child development and we aim to plan activities and resources that will promote and support them in our setting.

There are many benefits for playing in this way. Superhero and weapon play:

- Offers a great context for imaginative play, fantasy and creativity.
- Provides opportunities for children to develop detailed storylines and narratives.
- Engages even very shy children in exciting storylines.
- Presents children with opportunities to problem solve and resolve conflict.
- Provides opportunities to practise self-regulation and develop emotional intelligence.
- Helps children to explore the triumph of good over evil.
- Offers opportunities to discuss sensitive issues such as death, killing and gender stereotyping with children.
- Opens up conversations with children about everyday superpowers that we can all foster, e.g. resilience, friendship and listening skills.
- Provides plenty of opportunities for both gross and fine motor skills, developing proprioception and is usually very physical and active.
- Presents engaging and imaginative contexts that educators can use to develop children's cognitive skills.

In the light of these and other benefits we embrace this type of play. We will do so while keeping your child's welfare paramount.

Part of our role as early childhood practitioners is to support and extend children's interests and fascinations. We acknowledge that sometimes children will show an interest in subjects that we as adults may find uncomfortable or even distressing, such as killing and death. We know that the best way to support children in their developing understanding of such topics is to allow them to explore these issues through their play and talk. We will use our professional judgement as to when to intervene or when to remain observing.

We will ensure that any children engaging in energetic physical play are doing so under their own will and that any play fighting does not cross the line into violence. Observing children and paying close attention to what they say and do is part of our everyday practice here and thus we will closely supervise children if they engage in superhero play, rough and tumble play or other physical games. We will discuss with children the rules of playing in this way, set boundaries with them and remain vigilant in our care for your child.

Please do talk to us if you have any questions or concerns about this, or any of our policies. We will formally review this policy in six months' time and, in the meantime, will monitor our practice as we supervise the children on a daily basis.

Thank you for your continued support.

I have understood this policy.

Signed ....
Date ....

Appendix 2: Traditional heroes and villains

This list is not intended to be exhaustive or even very detailed – many characters have histories going back as much as 80 years and are frequently being reinvented, so it would be impossible to summarise them here.

Superhero Name ***Real-life name***	***Universe/Group***	***Hero/ villain***	***Superpower***	***Brief backstory/context***
Ant-Man Dr Hank Pym, later Scott Lang	Marvel Occasional member of the Avengers	Hero	Wears a suit that shrinks him to the size of an ant (and later grow to giant size). Wears a helmet that allows him to communicate with and control ants	Originally an invention of Dr Hank Pym, Ant-Man. Worked with the Wasp (Janet van Dyne), the two later married. More recently, Scott Lang (a reformed criminal), steals a suit from Pym and becomes the new Ant-Man. Pym and van Dyne's daughter, Hope, becomes the new Wasp
Aquaman Arthur Curry / Orin	DC Comics Member of the Justice League of America	Hero	Superhuman strength and the ability to breathe underwater	Defends the underwater kingdom of Atlantis and works with other members of the Justice League
The Avengers	Marvel	Heroes		The Avengers are a group of superheroes from the Marvel Comic Universe. Membership varies, but often includes Ironman, Thor, Captain America, Hulk, Black Widow, Hawkeye, Falcon and Scarlet Witch
Batgirl Barbara Gordon	DC Comics Justice League	Hero	Skilled at martial arts, highly intelligent	Sometimes appears alongside Batman. Several others have used the Batgirl name in the past, each with a different backstory In recent times, a teenage Batgirl appears as a member of the Young Justice League and the DC Superhero Girls

continued

. . . continued

Superhero Name ***Real-life name***	***Universe/Group***	***Hero/ villain***	***Superpower***	***Brief backstory/context***
Batman Bruce Wayne	DC Comics Justice League	Hero	Known for his impressive array of gadgets and vehicles and sidekick Robin	One of the earliest superheroes, originally created in the 1930s. Bruce Wayne witnessed his parents being murdered and this inspired him to fight crime. Despite growing up as an orphan, he went on to become a rich and successful businessman in Gotham City who uses his wealth to create gadgets and vehicles to fight crime. Usually portrayed as a dark and brooding character
Batwoman Katherine (Kate/ Kathy) Kane	DC Comics		Genius, skilled at martial arts and also has high-tech gadgets	Inspired by Batman, this wealthy heiress uses her money to fight crime in Gotham City
The Beast Henry Phillip "Hank" McCoy	Marvel X-Men Occasional member of Avengers and Defenders	Hero	Genius with ape-like superhuman physical strength and agility	Father was exposed to intense nuclear radiation at work which caused Hank to be born a mutant with long arms and legs and huge hands and feet. The Beast continues to mutate and becomes more "animal like" in form
Black Panther T'Challa	Marvel The Avengers	Hero	Strength and abilities are enhanced by exposure to a mystical herb	King of a fictional African country, the Black Panther role is passed down from father to son
Black Widow Natasha Romanoff	Marvel The Avengers	Hero	Highly skilled at martial arts and weaponry	Former Russian assassin, now fights alongside American superheroes the Avengers
Captain America Steve Rogers	Marvel The Avengers	Hero	Superhuman strength and resilience, enhanced with serum to be a "super soldier"	Rejected as a WW2 soldier for being too small, took part in an experiment to create a "super soldier". Frozen in time after the war, thawed out to join the Avengers

Cyclops Scott Summers	Marvel X-Men	Hero	Shoots powerful rays of energy out of his eyes controlled by a special visor	Born as a mutant with superhuman powers, Scott and brother Alex (Superhero Havok) become orphaned as their parents' plane is attacked by aliens. Their parents strap the only parachute onto the boys and they are saved from the crash. Scott is unable to control his powers without the special eyewear
DC Superhero Girls	DC	Heroes		A younger group of iconic superheroes like Batgirl, Supergirl, Wonder Woman and Harley Quinn (in this guise appearing as a hero rather than a villain). Created for younger audiences, the heroes attend Superhero High School and navigate the trials and tribulations of teenage life. Additional heroes include Bumblebee, Katana and Poison Ivy. Villains include Cheetah, Granny Goodness, Female Furies, Lena Luthor, Dark Opal and Eclipso Giganta
Doctor Strange Dr Stephen Strange	Marvel The Avengers	Hero	Sorcerer. Able to manipulate space and time. Wears a magical cape	Talented neurosurgeon, damaged his hands in a car accident. Learnt a form of sorcery in Tibet to enable his mind to heal his body. As a result, he now has the ability to manipulate space and time
Falcon Samuel Thomas Wilson	Marvel The Avengers	Hero	Excellent bird trainer, can see through eyes of birds and links telepathically with pet falcon. Skilled martial artist and gymnast Flies using mechanical wings	First African-American superhero in mainstream comics. Happy childhood, encounters racism in youth, both parents are killed within a couple of years of one another and Samuel becomes angry and bitter and is villain-like in nature. Later becomes one of the Avengers and fights many times alongside Captain America

continued

. . . continued

Superhero Name ***Real-life name***	***Universe/Group***	***Hero/ villain***	***Superpower***	***Brief backstory/context***
Fantastic Four **Mr Fantastic:** Dr Reed Richards **Invisible Girl/ Woman:** Sue Storm **Human Torch:** Johnny Storm **The Thing:** Ben Grimm	Marvel	Heroes	Mr Fantastic can stretch his body to extraordinary proportions Invisible Girl can make herself invisible and also project force fields and protective shields Human Torch can turn his whole body to fire The Thing became a huge rock-skinned creature	Exposed accidentally to cosmic rays, the four discovered they had developed special powers. Sue and Johnny are siblings, Sue and Reed marry, Reed and Ben are good friends, so the group is much like a family. Just to complicate matters, there have been other members of the Fantastic Four over the years.
The Flash	DC Comics	Hero	Super speed, superhuman reflexes and can violate laws of physics	Several heroes have been nicknamed the Flash over the years due to their ability to have super-speed
Green Arrow Oliver Queen	DC Justice League	Hero	Skilled at archery and martial arts	A wealthy young man, Queen was shipwrecked on a desert island. He made himself a bow and taught himself to use it. On returning to civilisation he used his new-found skills to fight inner-city crime
Green Lantern Hal Jordan	Marvel	Hero	Wears a ring of power, which enables him to create anything from his imagination	Pilot Jordan discovers a crashed spaceship containing a dying alien. The alien passes him a ring of power, which enables him to change his thoughts into reality There have been a number of different incarnations of Green Lantern over the years, but Hal Jordan is the most recent

Guardians of the Galaxy	Marvel	Heroes	Skilled fighters with a great soundtrack	A team of spacefaring superheroes, consisting of Star-Lord (Peter Quill, a human), Rocket Raccoon (a talking racoon), Gamora ("the deadliest woman in the whole galaxy"), Drax the Destroyer (a super-strong fighter) and Groot (a walking, talking tree). Although the characters existed individually for a long time, they were not brought together as a team until 2008
Harley Quinn Dr Harleen Quinzel	DC Superhero Girls	Villain (hero in DC Superhero Girls)	Gymnast, highly intelligent, immune to toxins	Worked at Arkham Asylum as a psychiatrist, fell in love with the Joker and helped him escape, becoming his accomplice and girlfriend. As part of DC Superhero Girls, Harley Quinn is depicted a hero rather than a villain; as a fun-loving class clown, carrying out pranks on her friends
Havok Alex	Marvel X-Men	Hero	Absorbs energy and turns it into plasma, controlled by a special suit	Born as a mutant with superhuman powers, Alex and his brother Scott (superhero Cyclops) become orphaned as their parents' plane is attacked by aliens. Their parents strap the only parachute onto the boys and they are saved from the crash. Alex has huge powers that he finds it difficult to control
Hawkeye Clint Barton	Marvel The Avengers	Hero	Skilled at archery, acrobatics and martial arts	Orphan Barton grew up in the circus, learning archery acrobatics, martial arts and many other skills. He used his skills to fight crime as Hawkeye, later becoming a regular member of the Avengers
Incredible Hulk Dr Bruce Banner	Marvel The Avengers	Hero	Superhuman size and strength	Bruce was a nuclear physicist, exposed to gamma radiation while saving a passer-by who wandered onto a testing site. As a result, Bruce can now turn into the Hulk (a huge green monster)

continued

... continued

Superhero Name ***Real-life name***	***Universe/Group***	***Hero/ villain***	***Superpower***	***Brief backstory/context***
Ironman Tony Stark	Marvel The Avengers	Hero	Genius, created a suit with a wealth of powers such as flight, super-strength and various weapons	A self-described "genius billionaire playboy philanthropist", Tony was an arms dealer turned superhero. He uses his technological genius and large amounts of money to make his Ironman suits and numerous other gadgets
The Joker Jack Napier	DC	Villain	Genius mind	A homicidal maniac and enemy of Batman. A chemical incident turned his hair green, his skin white and gave him a permanent wide red mouth, giving him the appearance of a clown
Lex Luthor	DC	Villain	Genius mind	Immensely intelligent, rich and powerful enemy of Superman
Loki	Marvel	Villain	Can assume the form of anyone he chooses, god-like strength and powers	Originating in Norse mythology, where he is the god of mischief, the supervillain character of Loki is portrayed as a shapeshifting trickster. He is brother to Thor by adoption and has been known to assist him at times, but is generally on the opposing side
Magneto Max Eisenhardt	Marvel	Villain and occasional hero	Can control magnetic fields	Born as a mutant with superhuman powers, Magneto wants to create a world in which mutants are the dominant species. This has brought him into conflict with the X-Men and his friend, Professor X. Sometimes portrayed as a hero and at other times as a villain

Marvel Girl/ Phoenix Jean Grey	Marvel X-Men	Hero	Telepathy, telekinesis	Born as a mutant with superhuman powers, Jean has a stable and loving home life and finds her powers when her best friend is killed when hit by a car. Recruited into X-Men as Marvel Girl and when in trouble later is saved as the Phoenix Force takes over her body and she becomes Phoenix
Professor X Prof Charles Xavier	Marvel X-Men	Hero	Telepathy, telekinesis	Leader of mutant team the X-Men, wheelchair-bound Professor X is a highly intelligent telepath, able to connect with and control other people's minds. Using a machine called Cerebro, he can find and connect with anyone on the planet
Quicksilver Pietro Maximoff	Marvel X-Men The Avengers	Hero	Super speed	Backstory has changed several times. Father is possibly Magneto and mother escapes while pregnant and gives birth to twins Wanda (Scarlet Witch) and Pietro. In some stories, Quicksilver is portrayed as a villain
Robin/Boy Wonder Dick Grayson	DC Teen Titans	Hero	Trained acrobat, skilled at martial arts	Robin grew up in the circus, where his parents were both performers and learnt to be an acrobat from a young age. When his parents were killed, he was adopted by Bruce Wayne (Batman), who trained him in combat. They worked together to fight crim in Gotham City. Robin later moved away from Batman to work with the Teen Titans
Rogue/Raven Anna Marie	Marvel X-Men	Hero (initially a villain)	Ability to absorb abilities, memories, personality, and physical characteristics of others by touching them	Grew up in a hippie commune in Mississippi, after her mother disappeared, her aunt looked after her and was very strict, which made Anna Marie rebel and run away. She saw her great powers as a curse and had to cover up to avoid touching anyone by accident

continued

... continued

Superhero Name ***Real-life name***	***Universe/Group***	***Hero/ villain***	***Superpower***	***Brief backstory/context***
Scarlet Witch Wanda Maximoff/ Frank	Marvel X-Men The Avengers	Hero	Sorcery, time, matter, probability and energy manipulation	Backstory has changed several times. Father is possibly Magneto and mother escapes while pregnant and gives birth to twins Wanda and Pietro. In addition to her mutant abilities, Wanda is given magical powers by the Elder god Chthon at birth. In some stories, Scarlet Witch is portrayed as a villain
Silver Surfer Norrin Radd	Marvel Occasional member of the Fantastic Four and the Avengers	Hero	Superhuman strength, endurance, rides silver surfboard at speed of light	The Silver Surfer was originally an astronomer (Norrin Radd) from planet Zenn-La and had to save his home from a villain called Galactus who devours planets to satisfy his hunger. He took some of Galactus's power and served him travelling faster than light on his surfboard. He is described as a humanoid with metallic skin and was later banished to earth after joining the Fantastic Four and preventing Galactus from consuming earth
Spider-Man Peter Parker	Marvel The Avengers	Hero	Super strength, agility, balance and ability to walk up vertical surfaces	Bitten by an irradiated spider, Parker acquires spider-like skills and abilities. Usually portrayed as a teenager or young adult, like many superheroes Parker is an orphan
Storm Ororo Munroe	Marvel X-men Occasional member of the Fantastic Four and the Avengers	Hero	Sorcery and ability to control the weather and atmosphere	First female black superhero. Parents were an African tribal princess and American photojournalist. Ororo descends from a long line of African witch-priestesses and is a mutant

Supergirl Kara Zor-El	DC Justice League	Hero	Superhuman strength and agility, flight, impervious to most weapons, laser eyes, freezing breath, x-ray vision, super-speed, and a sonic yell	Cousin to Kal-El (Superman), Kara was sent away from her home planet by her parents just before they, and it, were destroyed
Superman Kal-El/Clark Kent	DC Justice League	Hero	Superhuman strength and agility, flight, impervious to most weapons, laser eyes, freezing breath	An alien from the planet Krypton, Superman was sent to earth as a baby just before his home planet, including his family, was destroyed. Adopted by the humans who found him, he grew up as a human and moved to the city to work as a journalist. This enables him to keep track of crimes and incidents and always have a reason to be on site so that he can help
Thanos	Marvel	Villain	Superhuman strength, intelligence and speed, immortal, telepathic and can teleport	One of the most powerful villains in the Marvel universe, Thanos has come up against the Avengers, Guardians, X-Men and others. Many of the superheroes teamed up in an attempt to stop Thanos from acquiring the complete set of Infinity Stones, which would enable him to kill all humans
Thor	Marvel The Avengers	Hero	God-like powers of strength and endurance, immortal, can control the weather and uses Mjolnir, his magical hammer, as a weapon and for flight	Based on the Norse god of thunder, Thor now forms a regular part of the Avengers team. He comes to Earth to help defend against threats from other realms, especially where his brother Loki is involved
The Wasp Hope van Dyne	Marvel	Hero	Wears a suit that shrinks her to wasp size, can fly	See **Ant-Man**. Hope's mother was the original Wasp, working alongside original Ant-Man, her father Hank

continued

. . . continued

Superhero Name ***Real-life name***	***Universe/Group***	***Hero/ villain***	***Superpower***	***Brief backstory/context***
Wolverine James Howlett "Logan"	Marvel X-Men	Hero	Superhuman strength, speed and agility, able to regenerate his body, skeleton bonded with adamantium (indestructible metal), retractable claws	Wolverine is a mutant, whose ability to regenerate from any injury was utilised by a secret government programme, who bonded adamantium to his skeleton to make him virtually unbreakable. After a difficult past, he joined the X-Men, fighting for good. Ultimately quite a dark and complex character
Wonder Woman Diana of Themiscira/ Diana Prince	DC Justice League	Hero	Immortal, god-like strength, speed, intelligence, agility and flight. Skilled at weapons and hand-to-hand combat, can communicate with animals. Uses a lasso of truth, which binds enemies and makes them tell the truth. Flies in an invisible jet	Based on Greek mythology, Diana is the daughter of the Amazon queen Hippolyta. She grew up on Paradise Island, populated only by Amazon women. When Hippolyta was told that she must send a warrior to the world of man to protect and defend them, she held a contest but would not let her daughter, Diana, take part as she feared for her safety. Diana took part in secret and won. On earth, she assumed the identity Diana Prince
X-Men	Marvel	Heroes		A team of mutants led by Professor X. All have different powers and abilities and are often feared or reviled by non-mutants who seek to either control or eliminate them. Notable members of the team are Wolverine, Cyclops, Storm, Phoenix/Dr Jean Grey, Rogue and the Beast

Appendix 3: Children's heroic characters from cartoon and TV programmes

This chart contains a list of popular characters your children may have heard of or recognise. You may also remember characters from your youth such as Super Ted, Bananaman, He Man, She Ra and the Teenage Mutant Ninja Turtles who may reappear, get revamped or make a comeback. Many of the superheroes in Appendix 2 (e.g. Superman, Spider-Man, Batman) have cartoon versions of their adventures and comics and books aimed at younger viewers and readers. However, I have tried to avoid duplication and thus have omitted traditional heroes even if they fall into this category. This is not an exhaustive list. There is a fabulous website called commonsensemedia.org that aims to help parents and educators make informed decisions to enable children to "thrive in a world of media and technology". Do look it up!

Group *Name of hero*	*Superpower*	*Main enemies/ villains*	*Back story/context*
Ben 10 (Ben Tennyson)	Ability to transform into different aliens.	Various space aliens and supernatural entities	Ben acquires a watch-like alien device, the Omnitrix, which allows him to transform into 10 different alien creatures
Danger Mouse	World's greatest secret agent. He speaks 34 languages fluently, has the ability to shatter metal with his voice, perform military style push-ups on his index finger and reach a seventh level of meditation	The toad, Baron Silas von Greenback	Danger Mouse is a British secret agent who lives in a red pillar box outside the home of Sherlock Holmes in London. His sidekick, Penfold, is a hamster and they protect and save the world from impending peril with help from his boss Colonel K and the genius scientist Professor Squawkencluck
Danger Rangers **Sully**	Leader	Various villains including Rusty Ringtail, Worley the Weasel, Henri Ennui, Frinjas, Commander Octodon, Quentin V. Manderbill, Snarf and Knuckles.	This features animal heroes (Danger Rangers), their robot Fallbot and their artificial intelligence pal called SAVO (**S**afety **A**lert **V**ect**o**meter). The programme is designed to teach children about safety through examples and empower children with a "can-do" attitude, the power of adventure and the power to make smart choices. Catch phrase "Think Safe, Play Safe, and Be Safe"
Kitty	Intelligent, adventurous and resourceful		
Burble	Strong and safety expert		
Squeaky	Small, able to fix things on a small scale		
Burt	Creative inventor, personal safety expert		
Gabriela	Supervisor and head safety expert		

The Incredibles **Mr Incredible (Bob Parr)**	Invincible, super-strong	Syndrome Underminer Screenslaver (in film 2)	The Parr family (Mum, Dad and three children) live in suburbia but have secret identities and have to save the world from various supervillains. There have been two films so far, the first rated U the second PG
Elastigirl (Helen Parr)	Can stretch her body		
Violet	Invisibility and ability to create a forcefield around her		
Dash	super-speed		
Jack-Jack	Transmogrification (shapeshifting), heat vision, possibly more since, as he is still a baby he is just developing his powers		
Go Jetters **Xuli**	Pilot	Grand Master Glitch	The Go Jetters travel the world with their mentor and friend Ubercorn. They solve problems and save famous landmarks from the exploits of the villain Grand Master Glitch
Kyan	Gymnast		
Lars	Fixes things		
Foz	Clever		
Mighty Morphin Power Rangers Each series features a new group so there have been too many characters to list	Once "morphed", they have super-strength, durability, agility and combat skills. All Power Rangers have a weapon and some have additional superpowers, such as ESP or invisibility	As each series is about a new set of rangers, there have been too many villains to list	Power Rangers are normal teenagers who are recruited and trained by a mentor to morph into a Power Ranger Team. Each character wears a skin-tight coloured suit and helmet and has a weapon. There is always a red and blue ranger in each group and usually a yellow ranger, with other colours featuring in different series. The storyline in each series is independent of previous series

continued

. . . continued

Group *Name of hero*	*Superpower*	*Main enemies/ villains*	*Back story/context*
Numberjacks Numerals 0–9 are the individual characters	They have super-maths skills like number power, logical thinking and the ability to problem solve	The Meanies who consist of Problem Blob, the Puzzler, the Numbertaker, Shape Japer and Spooky Spoon	The Numberjacks are 10 small superhero numbers: 0, 1, 2, 3, 4, 5, 6, 7, 8 and 9. They live inside a sofa and real-life child agent calls on their help to solve maths problems. The Numberjacks work out a solution and always thwart their enemies, the Meanies
Octonauts **Captain Barnacles**	Captain, very strong, can drive any vehicle	No villains – they rescue creatures from impending peril, often created by natural causes	The Octonauts are a team of underwater explorers whose motto is "Explore – Rescue – Protect!" They live in the Octopod, an underwater base and have a fleet of aquatic vehicles. They are assisted by several vegimals, who Tunip leads. They help sea creatures in trouble and share various factual information about marine life throughout the programmes
Kwazii	Lieutenant and cryptozoologist		
Peso	Medic		
Professor Inkling	Oceanographer and founder		
Shellington	Biologist		
Tweak	Engineer		
Dashi	Computer programmer and photographer		
Tunip	Vegimal (half-animal, half-vegetable), chef and horticulturist		
PJ Masks **Catboy (Connor)**	Super-hearing, can jump high and far and has super speed	Romeo Lunar Girl Night-ninja Wolfy Kids	Connor, Amaya and Greg are six year olds who turn into superheroes at night to prevent various villains from ruining people's day. Most episodes also feature PJ Robot and Armadylan who help them save the day
Owlette (Amaya)	Super-sight and super-owl wing wind		
Gekko (Greg)	Camouflage, super-gekko muscles, super-lizard grip and super-lizard water run		

Powerpuff Girls **Blossom (pink)** **Bubbles (blue)** **Buttercup (green)**	All girls can fly, have super-strength, speed, x-ray vision, superhuman senses, energy projection, invisibility, and control over lightning and fire. Each girl also has additional superpowers that they use during the episodes	Lots of villains but main enemy is Mojo Jojo	Set in the fictional US city of Townsville, the series features three kindergarten-aged girls who fight various villains and monsters with an array of superpowers. The opening sequence explains that the girls were created by Professor Utonium in an attempt to create the "perfect little girl" however, he accidentally spilled "Chemical X" into the mixture which gave them all superpowers
Super WHY! **Whyatt Beanstalk**	Power to read	No villains, just problems to solve using literacy skills	The characters live in Storybook Village and each episode have to solve a problem that involves using their literacy skills. At the end Whyatt says, "Hip hip hooray! The Super Readers saved the day!"
Pig	Alphabet power		
Little Red Riding Hood	Word power		
Princess Pea	Spelling power and has a magic wand		
Team Unizoomi **Milli (sister of Geo)**	Pattern power (changes her dress pattern) and super-measuring skills (measures with her pigtails)	The security mouse (DoorMouse) of Umi City is their Frenemy and often gets in the way of their tasks. The Troublemakers (Little Trouble and Big Trouble) cause havoc and Team Unizoomi have to stop them	American animation that encourages children to have "Mighty Math Powers"! Based in Umi City, the characters have to solve problems and complete mathematical quests or tasks to help children in need
Geo (brother of Milli)	Creates objects with geometric shapes		
Bot (Green robot and friend of Milli and Geo)	Arms and legs can be extended to reach things, receives calls and has a screen on his tummy		

continued

. . . continued

Group *Name of hero*	*Superpower*	*Main enemies/ villains*	*Back story/context*
Thunderbirds **Jeff Tracy** **Scott** **John** **Virgil** **Gordon** **Alan**	No superpowers as such, very high-tech equipment and vehicles	The Hood	International Rescue (IR) is a secret organisation that aims to save humankind. It is made up of the Tracy family (Jeff Tracy and his five sons) and based on Tracy Island in the South Pacific Ocean. They have various high-tech vehicles that they use in their missions, named Thunderbird 1, 2, 3, 4 and 5. Other characters include Brains, Lady Penelope and Parker. The TV series was filmed using puppets
Tree Fu Tom	Uses movement (Tree Fu) to summon "Big World Magic" powers from the viewers at home	The Mushas (Puffy and Stink)	Tom is a boy with the power of movement magic – tree fu – which can transform him into an insect-sized superhero. He travels to Treetopolis, an enchanted kingdom and has adventures with his friends
Veggie Tales and Larryboy adventures **Larryboy (Cucumber)**	Plungers that shoot from his ears	Mother Pearl Greta Von-Gruesome Alchemist Awful Alvin	Larry works as a caretaker for the *Daily Bumble* newspaper in Bumblyburg and tries to manage his life as a superhero while working

Index

Locators in **bold** refer to tables.

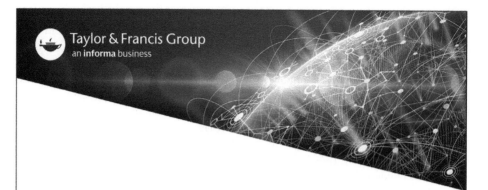

Milton Keynes UK
Ingram Content Group UK Ltd.
UKHW050732160224
437924UK00003B/4

9 781138 556973